A Feathering of Wisdom

An Inspired Life

When goals go, meaning goes,
When meaning goes, purpose goes.
When purpose goes,
Life goes dead on our hands.
Carl Jung 1875-1961

Anita Clara Iussa

A Feathering of Wisdom

Contents

Suburban Adelaide 2014 – 2015

Country Victoria   2000 – 2005

Photographs   *pages 64-65, 100-101*

References   *page 142*

Acknowledgements   *page 142*

Suburban Adelaide 2014 – 2015

Lessons from the Pidge

I don't know everything about pigeons but I do know they have qualities easily missed if not given some attention. I have much in common with pigeons, well, for a start, they're immigrants, like me. Like me they've learnt to live in this country we call Australia. While learning to behave accordingly we've adapted and developed certain sensitivities to our new environment.

Initially timid or suspicious of other varieties claiming the territory long before their arrival, pigeons back off a little and become observers. But as time goes on, they timidly take what they need for fear of offending, then with confidence boosted assert and even boast their command of the terrain.

I quite like having them visit my garden in suburban Adelaide. I call them pigeons but they're really turtle-doves, smaller and more impressionable than their larger, noisier and messier counterparts. These petite fussy versions *strut their stuff* like miniature fowls who've just laid eggs. Not only have they defended their right to be in my garden, they've cooed their way into my heart.

I have an affinity with these birds who love to canoodle and take umbrage to any of their kind getting in the way of connubial rites. Each has a unique personality but, invariably, all succumb to the demands of a certain pigeon with a proud demeanour and certain feistiness.
Easily distinguishable in his flock, he's the one demanding the right of recognition. Compelled to give him a name I have simply called him Pidge.

He is worthy of recognition because he's succeeded in doing what others have failed to do – lure me into periods of reflection to reveal what I may not have considered in my foray into semi-retirement.

Some people think birds come and go, taking what they need and never returning. Not so! Unlike friends who sometimes drift from our lives, despite our intentions of goodwill, their departure taking us by surprise. Pidge and the many feathered friends who visit keep me enthralled. They stay for the duration or at least until circumstances change. I understand and forgive them for not returning if the bird bath is empty, or the usual random seeds aren't scattered on the ground, or the sprinkler doesn't provide a welcome cool shower in hot days, or plants have withered and no longer give acceptable shelter.

I've learnt many lessons from Pidge but what I treasure most is the one about truly living each moment. He has reminded me that flexibility, adaptability and resilience in the face of unexpected change is a good thing. Pidge and his visiting feathered friends have allowed me to procrastinate purposely and embrace the wisdom of reflection to enable the past to release gracefully.

Destiny
Destiny is our will, and our will is nature. Disraeli

29th March 2014

Despite the many interruptions in my life, my path, in the universal scheme of things, may still have led me here to this point where I sit under my pergola on a comfy cane settee, quite cheap from a charity shop. Changes, mostly unexpected, happen when I'm focused and happily on track. Whether large or small is insignificant, it is what it is, an intrusion! This time it's the pigeons in for their daily seed. Not quietly waiting, but edging, strutting towards me, demanding what they now think is their right. Cooing noisily, they insist I pay them their dues. Have I set myself up for this by giving too freely? Probably. I resist. Enough is enough! I'll feed you when I'm ready.

Why does life have so much change in it!? I find myself here this year, where will I be next year? I've lost count of all my moves. Some people live in the same home all their lives and nothing seems to change for them. Am I grumbling, no, just remembering the strain of it all?! Setting up again always brings me a sense of excitement, a thrill and a scariness too; a new environment, a different home, décor, new domestic and work routines demanding more focused attention. I thrive on the creativity involved. Change from the inside out is much more challenging, and frightening, since my mind and heart come with me wherever I go burdened with the dregs of the past, while the new demands commitment and stamina.

My undisclosed destiny, the real issue now I'm sixty-five, is knocking at the door. What *am* I doing sitting here doing nothing? I'm trying to prepare for retirement and getting older, that's what! But I'm not doing so well. How do I let go of the full-on years of teaching and helping others, my life's work, and still support myself financially and emotionally in this otherworldly life I live?

In recent days I've resisted putting pen to paper. Too much to write about – people, places, feelings to digest and put out of my life. The last eighteen months have been intense. So that I can reclaim my life in this little unit, a stone's throw from the beach, I'm taking a feather from Pidge's cap and managing to put challenges and problems on hold and be *here* now.

While the physical environment demanded jaunts to opportunity shops to find treasures for this cosy one-bedroom home, the mystical garden and its tiny inhabitants have anchored me and offered moments of magic. Under my pergola I have a *bird's eye-view* of my world as an observer of life, a role I've been comfortable in for as long as I can remember, and the times before remembering, so my parents tell me. At age three they worried because I hadn't started to talk, instead I'd sit and survey my surroundings, quietly watching what was going on.

Pigeons come to eat and drink along with a menagerie of other birds who I've come to recognise by calls and twitters. They hide in the fronds of the jacaranda, a majestic tree owning a third of my back yard. I admit, almost guiltily, I can't quite take to the wattle bird with its raucous sound. Why its regarded as a honeyeater is beyond me – probably belongs to the dinosaur age, an enigma, timid and clumsy. My favourites are the New Holland honeyeaters, small, yellow and black who launch in flurries into the last few summer flowers with charming, light laughter. They love the crimson and pink dominating most of the garden. I had no idea hollyhocks could be so resilient, withstanding not only the weather but onslaughts of a number of birds landing on them to sample the honeyed treats. One day a group of finches fluttered joyfully into the blooms bending the stem to the ground with their combined weight then releasing it to spring upwards. Then repeating it all over again like a wonderful game!

Under the jacaranda there's a fairy garden where I've tried to apply my creative touches. But my granddaughter doesn't think it measures up to her standards! Now five, she knows that fairy gardens have little organisation, they just happen – a gnome here, fairies in trees or bushes, the ceramic piglet with a crown we bought together at yet another charity shop and princesses, anywhere. Her older brother whose pursuits are different is drawn into her imaginary games involuntarily. A run along the stepping stones from one end of the garden to the other, repeated several times, perhaps escaping from imaginary pursuers. His inquisitive mind alert and insatiable loves pondering on historical facts. His knowledge of things historical at age eight far surpasses mine. I try to distract him with unrelated topics or ply him with stories of my childhood and things he normally shies away from. Food easily does the trick distracting him from any number of things. I call him *our gastronome*.

The other day the fairies and princesses formed an army. But he was prepared. He'd gathered his dinosaurs and other bits and pieces I'd bought on my last trip to the charity shop and *called the shots*. Proclaiming his control of the territory his sister eventually, and reluctantly, *towed the line*. There was an explosion of towers and flags on twigs and bamboo garden stakes. He didn't have enough *soldiers,* he needed *more men,* he said. We gathered small sticks to make bodies and held their arms and legs together with rubber bands and sticky tape – he was happy.

Retirement
He who lives wisely to himself and in his own heart
looks at the busy world through loopholes of retreat,
and does not want to mingle in the fray. Hazlitt

30th March, 2014

Already the activity outside my bedroom rises to a gentle crescendo. Large and small birds stirring, fluttering, warbling, the sound of next-door breakfast-making and the faint hum of traffic imbue the air with morning energy. The cooing of Pidge is unmistakeable and alerts me to the duties of a new day, and the seeds I've unwittingly promised.

One of my long-term yoga students, on the way to being a close friend, will arrive in a couple of hours and we'll be on our way to Middleton down south. A South Australian retreat for yoga students, interestingly, will be in the seaside township where I held my first retreat on returning from Victoria in 2005. Quite different from the rural retreats held in my country property Sundarra where I made use of our homestead while my then husband worked away. The accommodation consisting of rudimentary live-in arrangements, bunk beds, a reorganised spacious living area to make way for two tables and chairs, enough for eight, and acres and acres of nature.

I needed to earn money. The property had a bottomless pit and anything earned disappeared into it for maintenance jobs, the running of the place, infrastructure and the sizeable mortgage. The homestead, positioned in the centre of the property, like an island in the middle of bushland fringed by neighbours' land on one side and the Bonyaricall Creek and the Murray Valley Highway on the other, was a strange shape, almost a perfect triangle. Week nights sleeping in a single bed in the smallest room surround by empty bedrooms uninvited guilt would creep into me, *here I am in this empty house with so much space while many others are homeless.*

Our homestead had lost its heart when my husband left for a new job, three hour's drive away, returning only on weekends. I needed to fill the place with people, warmth and laughter and share my beautiful land, its creatures, sunrises and sunsets and the wind in the trees who spoke to me with voices of the ancients, my unseen companions.

Relieved that that part of my life together with its pain and beauty is over, I embrace my new beginning in this pocket of land in the suburbs wholeheartedly. Today at Middleton I'll check out the holiday home where I'll hold the retreat, something I hadn't envisaged on the horizon. Running retreats in Adelaide was never in my planning, especially on my journey to retirement; it arose unexpectedly courtesy of one of my yoga students – a time of rest and recovery for a handful of long-term students keen for some respite from daily living.

Folly
The wise man knows himself to be a fool. Shakespeare

1ˢᵗ *April 2014*

Today its summer again. Like me it hasn't quite learnt to let go of what has been and tugs and pushes constantly until autumn wins. As I sit in my garden with the cooing pigeon and feathered friends, and the machinery in the vacant block thankfully fading into the background, I cannot but think that every piece of land is beautiful.

This suburban dot of land, unlike the vast property I left behind years ago, patiently waited for me to find its beauty aided by the unexpected find of a feathered friend. It would have been foolhardy not to have noticed that Pidge has a personality above any other of his flock. Bold and quirkily fluffing his wings at me demanding attention, (or is it the bird seed), he's managed to anchor me, draw me into his little environment giving me permission to observe and reflect.

The first of April is not just another day, it brings back joys of things long forgotten. I was on the receiving end of school friends' tricks, embarrassed at first then laughing as I saw the funny side of things. That humour has remained with me, a little slow to catch on sometimes but always in for a good laugh though I may be on the receiving end.

The April first in the year 2000 was my wedding day, another one, and another folly. We married on the rural property we bought together and named Sundarra – a Sanscrit word meaning *beautiful one.* The land extended to a tiny tributary off the River Murray, the Bonyaricall Creek.

My youngest son and my husband's two daughters shared the drive for the day, a five-hour trip from Melbourne, and seemed to have got on like a house on fire by the time they arrived. My eldest son and fianceé arrived from Adelaide. We'd snuck in our wedding literally weeks before theirs at the end of the month. It was meant to be an intimate gathering, but the marriage celebrant and her husband stayed on and on, and on, inviting themselves to our simple family breakfast barbecue, despite our hinting that their part of the proceedings was over! The whole affair was hilarious from beginning to end.

On the way to the wedding site, the banks of the Bonyaricall Creek, our mode of transport was a Ute. We sat *regally* on the back tray top in canvas chairs tied down securely to limit movement as it meandered along the rough dirt track to the creek minutes away. Other family members were squashed into the cabin of the Ute next to my eldest son, the designated driver. We whooped and laughed hysterically holding onto our rickety chairs as the Ute ploughed through the uneven sun-dried terrain to its destination.

The colour theme was red and black hastily thrown together for the day. A long black evening gown, the only elegant thing in my then country wardrobe, set off with a three-quarter length red dress-coat and a bouquet of red bottle brush, picked as an afterthought from our ramshackle bush garden, was the only other adornment. He wore a red Turkish Fez hat, embellished with the Mallee dust shared copiously with other strange memorabilia displayed in a little alcove of our homestead. A red matching bow tie with white shirt and red cummerbund atop black trousers completed the look.

The ceremony, drawn together not so much by our promise to honour each other but to make a pledge to the land, had no romance. We promised to guard and protect it for future generations. I'd spent a great deal of time planning the format and my part of the ceremony but in the moment when we expressed our *intent* toward each other I realised my husband-to-be hadn't planned anything. I read a poem I'd written soon after we met – something about finding himself a survivor on the shores of life. He read a verse from an unidentified poem that to this day I can't remember or at the time even understood. It came crumpled from his pocket and went straight back in after he'd read it – a stanza from some heroic epic, nothing to do with us or the land we'd pledged to protect. The only significantly *wedding* part was the *I do*. Yes, a truly memorable April Fool's Day!

It's been said your heart goes with you wherever you go, but, when I returned to Adelaide, I knew my heart hadn't travelled with me. Somehow, I've managed to prise it from Sundarra and its spectacular Mallee country and put it into this back garden – my home, my solitary place, a small pocket of nature in the suburbs.

Belief
*To believe is to be happy; to doubt is to be wretched.
To believe is to be strong. Doubt cramps energy. Belief is power.
Only so far as man believes strongly, mightily, can he act cheerfully,
or do any thing that is worth doing.* F. W. Robertson

5*th* April 2014

I sit under the pergola intent on enjoying the garden and quieting my nervous energy by doing something useful at the same time. With an array of photos and forgotten treasures scattered around me I look for the card my youngest son sent me for a late fortieth birthday.

The garden watered, the customary bird seed spread but with other domestics still demanding my attention I only intend to search for that one thing; one item after the other comes out for examination from the box I'd commandeered from the garden shed. While berating myself for taking so long to complete the task, I reminisce over every letter, birthday card, photo and a host of paraphernalia no longer having a place in my life or my retirement.

Finally, in the plastic sleeve among an assortment of cartoon pictures, a fully illustrated story about creatures in outer space only an eight-year-old could have written, postcards and emails he'd sent on his first overseas trip, I find it. The birthday card boasts a black and white photo of a figure leaping across a chasm at Stand Rock, Wisconsin. I have no idea where that is, and never bothered to check it out on a map. Reading it anew, decades after he'd written it, only twenty-two years old, it is not just funny and witty but a poignant and wise contribution to my life.

He'd begun with, well, its birthday time again, but we're not actually going to mention age or *anything irrelevant like that. As Lady*

Bracknell says: "London society is full of women of the very highest birth who have, of their own free choice, remained thirty-five for years. Lady Dumbleton is an instance in point. To my knowledge she has been thirty-five ever since she arrived at the age of forty, which was many years ago now." and concludes with, *Take that leap!*

And so it was, on his advice, regardless of age, when my school teaching career ended and I was contemplating a new career, I took *that leap*. Through professional development courses in the education system, I'd studied the intricacies of *stress* and how best to manage it, in an effort to dissuade the hungry monster from gobbling me up completely. My son's birthday card initiated the many great leaps I was to take in my life. The first of which was to run a wellness practice from home, no overheads, working in my way, my hours, and when and how I wanted until I recovered from teacher-stress overload.

Still in the business of education I now taught what was intimately close to my experience, stress, and how to manage it. This included teaching life skills and developing the confidence to take risks. Three years on I took another gigantic jump into the unknown and left Adelaide to establish a wellness retreat centre on an isolated 712-acre property bordered by the River Murray in north-west Victoria. Both my sons were impressed by the move for different reasons; the eldest with his passion for freshwater fishing, especially Murray River cod, saw it as an opportunity for frequent visits. While the younger, seeing his mother take another leap of faith and yearning to work in the film and television industry, moved to Melbourne saying, 'If you can do it, I can do it!'

Until I rummaged in this box of memorabilia, undisturbed for years, the significance of that card and his words lay forgotten in my life. I now see the immense relevance of his wisdom in both our lives – he went on to many more leaps of faith in the film industry, Melbourne, Sydney and ironically America, the birthplace of that birthday card.

Meditation

Meditation is that exercise of the mind by which it recalls a known truth – as some kinds of creatures do their food, to be ruminated upon. Bishop Horne

6th April 2014

Inevitably the older I get the more experiences I accumulate. Life is no longer linear; it circles to parts I've already lived. Like the Pidge I circle back to ground I've already covered, hoping to pick up grains of truth and understanding I might have missed. In terms of my spiritual learnings, what's happened in the past should stay there and not concern me in the present, however, I find it useful to refer to past experiences which I like to call past lives, dormant memories begging to be reignited in my consciousness for inspection and introspection.

On the last day of a meditation teacher training course the senior tutor scrutinised the class and said categorically *if you cease meditation practice you will draw in the past…your mind will be attracted to many things and chatter incessantly.* I shuddered. Was he talking to me? Already overwhelmed with setting up my new counselling and yoga business requiring financial commitment, my in-depth meditation time had become limited. And it wasn't the only thing that concerned me, a new man had come into my life – the added pressure of changing my life to accommodate his unexpected presence was playing havoc with my peace of mind. He was insistent and would not be dismissed. After several years of an ordered, celibate life, here was this man pursuing me with great ardour.

At age 61 I didn't realise or even entertain the slightest thought I was attractive and desirable. My life was committed to teaching yoga and meditation arising from a well-grounded base formed over many years from the spiritual practices supporting my life's work which included stress management counselling.

It was becoming increasingly difficult to balance the physical, material world with the world I'd lived so long. When the meditation master teacher alluded to the replacement of meditation practice with other pursuits, in a room full of students I felt he was speaking only to me.

Opening up in this relatively new relationship was the possibility of sharing my life with someone who cared about me. This was not to be dismissed out of hand even though I tried to restrain my mind circling back to my April Fool's Day wedding which, unknowingly, was the beginning of the end of that relationship – my new husband becoming increasingly emotionally absent took to hiding in a little attic inside his head while the door to his heart remained firmly closed. Fortunately, the emotional isolation was replaced with the richness of nature, its vast embrace holding me in perpetual stillness on our bush property, an equivalent to endless daily meditation. Though physically isolated Sundarra was real, inviting me with spectacular sunrises into each day while the perpetually glowing sunsets wrapped around me and held me quietly and lovingly into the night.

Sundarra wasn't always like this. When I first moved in it was raucous, harsh, and, noisy. The transportable homestead perched in the centre of the property on concrete pylons a metre above the flood plain had no electrical power so we relied on a generator in an adjacent shed, three metres from our back door. The shed rattled and groaned reverberating with the noise of the old rattly generator which choked the air with diesel fumes. What I thought was going to be an oasis of peace became disturbing and distressing. The sweet times it was turned off my whole being sank into exhausted stillness, then, gradually replenished with meditation, I gathered myself together for the next onslaught. Solar power and a new quieter generator, used sparingly, came later.

Sunrise at Sundarra was resplendent, in every season. My favourite viewing platform was the top step, which the ingenious former owners had constructed from railway sleepers, outside the back door where I'd sit, cuppa in hand to watch the mist bring forth the sun. It was magical. This dot of a garden in the suburbs urges me to repeat what I've already lived. Every sunrise I come full circle on this wooden pergola with the straggly grapevine to contemplate life and watch the magic of each day unfold with my feathered friends.

Command
*It is better to have a lion at the head of an army of sheep,
than a sheep at the head of an army of lions.* De Foe

8th April 2014

A gentle rain which has been hovering for a few days breaks free. What a relief, my whole body responds. I love the sound, a symphony no human has ever been able to imitate seeps through the pores of my skin calming every sinew of tension in me. I want to sit here letting it soothe me forever. But, an appointment across town to view a hall for a yoga event demands my attention. The responsibility of looking for yoga workshop venues for our interstate team takes me out of my bullish tendencies to over-organise and attempt to take charge of things outside my control.

I watch the pigeons, a few stragglers who don't mind the rain, peck at the few remaining seeds. I must get some more today. Aah, that's the lesson! When you have a purpose and no definite plans just meander along picking up life's offerings and let someone else take command! As much control as we *think* we have, we really have none. At any moment, hours, days and weeks of planning can dissolve into nothingness.

All I've been told is that the yoga event will probably take place in November, at an unspecified date, with an undetermined number of people and an undecided format. *On a wing and a prayer* is how master yogis live. It's remarkable that with that kind of philosophy they've amassed considerable following around the world and manifested the physical means to run programs on wellness, yoga and meditation within a base of deep-seated spirituality for decades.

Rain
Be still, sad heart, and cease repining;
Behind the clouds the sun is shining;
Thy fate is the common fate of all, into each life some
rain must fall, some days must be dark and dreary. Longfellow

10th April 2014

The fledgling sun seeps through the clouds, though the two days of rain is easing it still cascades with great fervour. It had started gently this morning but it's now a steady downpour putting any thoughts of feeding Pidge to rest. My mother used to say that whenever a shower of rain fell while the sun still shone it was a sign of witches combing their hair. We never questioned her logic – this was part of Mammina's mystery. We preferred to marvel at the eccentricity of her life in a tiny village in the north-eastern part of Italy where seemingly all manner of strange things happened.

Mammina is no longer with us, well, not in the way she was before. She visits in the most amazing snippets of memory landing unexpectedly and with incredible ease into my life. Rain, hand in hand with vibrant sunshine in the early evening shower, cascades gently down the wide lounge room window overlooking the lawned common area in front of my little unit and suddenly, Mammina is here!

Mammina died two years ago and only now I've begun to miss her, maybe because I have the time to do so. Too much has happened in the last couple of years; closing my yoga and counselling studio, relocating to Kangaroo Island and setting up classes there, and, back again within two years. Only now I'm settling. She would have loved this place, enough garden to fossick around in and perhaps grow some veg. Mostly It's her silliness and sense of the ridiculous I miss. There should have been more of it! Maybe she thought that too! But life took hold of her and demanded she be an adult!

As I moved through teen years and into young womanhood my relationship with her was like target practice, sometimes it hit, often it missed. I felt challenged by limitations she placed on me – in the end this served to have an opposite effect. I became strongly independent and feasted on life's challenges, and there were many. I've heard it said that we choose our parents, not just our friends. In this context, I guess she gave me all I needed to survive in the world, mainly the ability to let go of what no longer served me so I could make a new start – in this instance, here with my feathered friends, relishing my independence and freedom to be who I am and to do what I do.

Passing
Every parting is a form of death;
as every reunion is a type of heaven.   T. Edwards

24th April, 2014

Tomorrow is Anzac Day. I wake disturbed from sleep by some unknown thing. A sudden noise from the next-door neighbours of the attached walls, or a gust of wind through the gigantic jacaranda dwarfing the garden.

A piece of toast and chai tea later I sit in bed contemplating whether to reset the alarm and have a snooze. The sun is still a long way off – maybe a look through some poems I'd been given by a nice young man I met on Kangaroo Island. He'd handed me one of his poems, *Worry Street*, some time ago – it was good, insightful – when he'd called in after his lawnmowing job for a cuppa I offered to read his poetry. A year later he sends me his poems inspiring me to write more of my own.

Tomorrow I'll go to the Anzac dawn service and stand in crisp autumn air with thousands of people and reflect on life, dying and glory. We'll gather at the War Memorial in North Terrace with a multitude of strangers while the huge angel, looking surreal in fledgling morning light with his long sword at rest, looks over us.

My new friend, a loyal yoga student invited me to the observance last year – his reverence for the whole affair took me outside my thoughts into a time warp of stillness. I stood shoulder to shoulder with strangers mourning the loss of human lives and basked in a strange gratitude for all things present. Having no expectation of the day apart from an early breakfast in one of the local cafes and wondering how we'd fill the time before the Anzac Day parade began, I was unprepared for what happened.

At a fast pace I was steered in the direction of the gardens in North Terrace, the corner opposite the Botanic Gardens. We stood on the footpath while others sprawled around us on the green verges and onto the road at the Australian Light Horse Memorial and horse troughs. Beyond, were an entourage of horses mounted by WW1 uniformed men who, I was told, were re-enacting the 9th Light Horse Regiment of Gallipoli together with regular soldiers incorporating The Royal Australian Armoured Corps in South Australia.

At this Australian Light Horse Remembrance Service, I learned of inconceivable wartime feats, the endurance of the Waler horses and the men who rode them in Gallipoli and throughout the Palestine Campaign. This ceremony, drawing people of all ages together to honour those steadfast, strong animals and their riders who'd saved many lives and endured up to their tragic end, was unexpectedly moving. There was no holding back tears when the strains of the National Anthem sung by a lilting young voice filled the cool morning air and the horses ambled to the water troughs where children fed them carrot treats.

I later learned that my friend's great uncle, a Light Horseman, tragically died and that it was against regulations to repatriate the surviving horses after the war. Soldiers, who'd become their companions were ordered to shoot them. Nonetheless, one story tells that some had been secreted away to local Turkish villages and their blood stock still remains. I want to believe this. Anzac Day has taken on a completely different meaning for me. Again, I want to be part of a humanity honouring the sacredness of life, of those who died in extraordinary circumstances, for purposes I don't completely understand.

Property
Exclusive property is a theft in nature. Brissot

31st May 2014

Just finished my cuppa and toast, a ritual I relish in the stillness of early morning. My birthday has come and gone with small degree of celebration. While the world changes around me the pigeon remains the same, strutting and eyeballing me puposely. He spots me behind the trailing autumn grapevine. The one without any fruit, only mold on what would have been grapes, now tiny and inedible – serves me right for counting the bunches before they hatched!

I've done the same with my yoga classes, few now I've closed my yoga studio. When I fill the hired hall with a yoga class, I'm happy. Taking in the numbers at a glance estimating if the current trend continues, I'll have enough to pay bills for another few weeks. Unfortunately, commitment is fickle when it comes to people caring for themselves – sustaining a yoga class regularly in the busyness of modern living is a feat only few manage.

The miniscule grapes have been eaten by birds, blackbirds mainly. I hear them trilling in that sweet time between wakefulness and sleep before the sun has decided to shine. Today, my precious little hideaway, after three weeks of noisy builders, gas fitters and council workers removing wild bamboo from the gully bordering my backyard, becomes a place of stillness again. No, I spoke too soon! An empty block in full view of my sacred space has landed a conclave of machinery. Someone has taken advantage of the seclusion among a myriad of trees thriving happily along the edge of the gully to build. Another disturbing sound rears its ugly head and becomes constant – an angle grinder from the next street stridently cutting into the stillness of my space – somebody's weekend pursuit. Yesterday, Sunday, it was punctuated by a neighbour's raucous indelicate language **F* F* F*!** Is this my quiet little hideaway? Do I really want to live in the suburbs!?

Thankfully a part of me remains undisturbed as I stoically sit in my favourite place until the noise fades. The garden watered the pigeon returns, or should I say pigeons. But the flock soon diminishes as the Pidge methodically asserts his territory with the choicest of bird language and domineering struts dispersing them into full flight. So, that's why his ample chest has a few ruffled feathers. Protecting territory is a full-time job. I know how he feels!

Eighteen months after my little jaunt on Kangaroo Island, this hideaway in the suburbs felt like a soothing balm. Again, I'd borne the brunt of poor choices and like Pidge, my feathers had been severely ruffled. My territory had been trespassed on and the territory was me. Have I learnt my lessons? I'm not sure, I only know not to lay claim on places and people.

Abundance
*Not what we have, but what we enjoy,
constitutes our abundance.* J. Petit-Senn

16th June 2014

I've lived, and am living, a full and complete life. Though certain things have troubled me and challenged my very existence I'd change nothing. Somehow everything has sorted itself out without my maximum control. What *has* worked is my ability to move from one situation to another by unconsciously applying *letting go* strategies. All kinds of toing and froing stages precede the final *letting go*. When the urge to be responsible for putting everything right in the past, present and future disappears, a wonderful sense of freedom follows.

Things around me in this spacious one-bedroom unit are testament to the abundance I continually receive. Could all of this have come about simply because I feed birds, mostly Pidge, always ready for a serve of his favourite seed? Well, I don't know, but one of my wise master yoga teachers was very big on feeding birds to create abundance!

My daily reflections invariably make me realise that it's not about how much I've done or achieved, but how I feel about what I've done and achieved. My ultimate goal to accept I've done the best I possibly could, undoubtedly contributes to the final *letting go* stage. As I begin the week this life philosophy sits strongly inside me. I'm convinced that the more *I let go* the more I let a greater planner do whatever is right for me at the time. Oh yes, I know about free will, I've used it constantly and pig-headedly, muddling along until I've learnt the wisdom to live well.

It's been quite cold in the mornings so I allow myself the indulgence of a cup of tea, a *dipping* biscuit and hop back into bed for a period of reflection. Invariably this sets me up for meditation in the cosiness of my pink blanket, a remnant of my mother's possessions, nestled in a bamboo-framed bed. The bed free, courtesy of the footpath one street over, I discovered on a regular walk to the local supermarket for a few essentials. There it was, discarded and unloved, a remarkably unique piece of furniture, larger than a single bed, more like a day bed. Returning with my sedan to transport it home was out of the question; the young woman in the next-door unit had a 4WD, maybe this was the go.

When I mustered up the courage to ask for help, she didn't look overjoyed but agreed to help out anyway. Soon we were trying to manoeuvre this heavy and unwieldy piece of furniture into the back of her car, with little success – too wide and too long. I thanked her and she left without a second glance. I surveyed this handsome bamboo treasure and with a throwaway thought glanced expectantly up the road, *What I need is a Ute.* I'm a firm believer in the power of positive manifestation but this was ridiculous – there it was, a Ute, pulling into the kerb. *Looks like you need a hand* the driver, like a knight in shining armour on his white steed, said as he jumped out of the vehicle.

Abundance continues despite changes of circumstance, house moves, wealth, relationships and so much more. Yes, financial stability has been elusive like a butterfly landing momentarily than flying off again before a situation completely steadies. But despite the changes, abundance has been constant in unexpected ways. Last year, days since I returned from Kangaroo Island, I relished the fact I was travelling lightly, in more ways than one; I needed to furnish my unit but was mostly unconcerned – my sparkling, spacious seaside unit was home again. Fresh-looking cane pieces sprang out of nowhere without blowing my meagre budget. Easily movable bamboo furniture from my favourite op shops – the shelving, desk and a settee making way for yoga classes in my spacious living room.

Once my steel-framed double-bed was replaced with the newly-sourced bamboo bed the bedroom became large enough to hold furnishings from the lounge room, my yoga space on certain days – a great way to immediately increase my income without extra overheads. I easily fitted seven yoga mats on the polished wooden floor. The cane furniture came from an Iranian second-hand dealer who called me *ma'am* with such respect and sensitivity I was convinced he was a meditator, maybe a Sufi. I bought wicker shelving units, a solid cane dresser with doors, a tea-for-two bamboo table with chairs and other items. He graciously delivered them, making an offer on my old bed which paid for delivery costs.

Within this spirit of *letting go* I live a life of abundance. I have no debts, owe nothing, material or otherwise, to anyone. What has happened between myself and others has been forgiven, at least on my part. I don't feel responsible for other's perception of the situations we've shared – they are theirs to deal with. I'm free to handle my life with flow and sincerity while trying not to attract anything inessential. There's constant movement, and at the same time stability in this little place I call *home*. Furniture, household items and people come and go freely and happily as needs arise.

Patience
Adopt the pace of nature: her secret is patience. Emerson

23rd June 2014

Pidge knows more about life and survival than I do. It's quite clear, *he* is the master of patience and I'm still in training. He's an adept in attracting what he needs for survival. I may marvel at how abundance fills my life, but like a fledgling learner there's a part of me that hasn't fully accepted that I'm its creator. When I glance up from the kitchen sink to look out of the window I see the jacaranda, loquat and surrounding tree canopies framed against the sky, and it's here, on a branch directly in front of the window that the pigeon sits, eyeballing me, compelling me to go outside, especially when it's cold and wet, to deliver his customary seed.

The window is a constant reminder for me to look up, to set my sights high and be grateful for the opportunity to do so. During one of my small group learning programs which I hold at home, one of the participants helping to clean the remains of a shared lunch at the sink said, *it's a pity, you can't see outside when you wash the dishes* and suggested I could make the window deeper, so that it was at eye level. I smiled and told her I liked it the way it was, my window to the sky.

One morning I find Pidge has discovered, yet again, where I am when I'm not sitting under the pergola or at the kitchen sink. I'm having a late start after a fitful sleep during a stormy night and sit with my morning cuppa in bed, reading. The timber venetian blind has been up since early light, and, eyeballing me, away from the windy branches of the jacaranda sits Pidge – he's found a cosy spot in the fronds of the frangipani bush neatly sheltered in a corner outside the window. He's brought his mate, as he does from time to time when he's in the mood to share some of his titbits. The master of patience, knowing that without fail the seed will appear, is waiting. Its far beyond my usual rising time and guiltily I resist the urge to go out into the windy rain-filled day. Meditation in this warm bed first, then outside activity.

How long will it take for me to settle completely into semi-retirement without feeling that I should rush around completing tasks? The *Taurus* in me resists the compulsion and finally, at peace with the pigeon's message, I practice the art of patience without condemnation!

Children
Children have neither a past nor a future;
and, what scarcely happens to us, they enjoy the present. Bruye`re

29th June 2014

Last Friday I picked the grandkids up from school, a much longed-for opportunity to enjoy their child's world again. My long-term yoga friend came with me this time. Gradually I'm giving myself permission to share part of my personal life with him – the second time in six months that he's shared time with the grandkids. The older boy has such special qualities with a penchant for details endearing him to quiet reflective thinkers, just like my friend who's becoming my steady companion. They fall into deep discussions, present and historical, of the world and our place in it. This time the conversation steeped into the arena of Australian sport and its heroes. We went off to a charity shop to buy some books; miraculously, what fell from the shelves was a spectacularly illustrated book of Aussie sport – what a bonus!

For his younger sister it's still all about fantasy, princesses, fairies and the colour pink. At age five and eight respectively, they are a great joy and full of unexpected reflections, imaginings and questions. Feeding the *princess* can be somewhat of a challenge, I've discovered. However, a good bowl of spaghetti and loads of tomato sauce topped with grated cheese does the trick. Grating vegetables into the sauce is not my preferred pastime, especially mushrooms, but together with sweet potato, and sometimes zucchini; with the tomatoes disguising the remnants of all vegetables it becomes a delicious and healthy meal.

The jobs, the small ones I've been putting off, demand my attention – three plastic boxes, contents ready for sorting, sit on the pergola decking.

A few more, squirrelled away in my miniscule garden shed drew my granddaughter's attention, *Nanita, your shed's so little* and adds, *I love your house, the toilet, laundry and bathroom are all together*. Satisfied that the garden was free of pigeons, which she'd chased away earlier, she continued in awed tones, *and your shower is over the bath.*

The siblings complement each other beautifully bringing together all the layered dimensions and differences in their personalities. Needless to say, the Pidge wisely keeps his distance when they're around, avoiding boisterous activity at all costs.

It's Sunday so the plan of catching up on emails makes way for the pleasure of catching the afternoon sun. At last, the rain has tired! Early rain has already fulfilled our winter quota. Twenty or more years ago, I knew the day of the week and the time without consulting a diary or a clock just by listening. Sitting here with the sun bobbing in and out of the jacaranda rhythmically to the continuous hum of traffic, I'm none the wiser, it could be any day of the week. The little court where my unit sits behind a manicured lawn common area is set well back from two main roads; in the middle of a triangle, so to speak.

In my childhood world Sundays were free of football matches because everyone went to church. Didn't they!? No shops to shop in and no large regular community events, except those of a religious nature or associated with churches.

On week days traffic eased off when shops closed and, on Saturday when afternoon football matches ended, especially at the time of year deemed too dark or too cold to be outside. *Am I old? I must be if I can look back on the 'good old days.'* I've always favoured peace, calm and quiet over frenetic activities, even as a child when writing poetry was a secret pleasure, a time when reflective thoughts helped me make sense of the world. Vitamin D, nature's gift, now so widely recommended by health professionals to older people, and in increasing numbers to younger ones, was once delivered naturally into our lives. Yes, life has changed a great deal with its busyness and the push and pull of modern technology.

Now heating and cooling is as easy as the touch of an app on a mobile phone before arriving home from wherever. Treats, such as home gyms, theatre rooms and heated indoor swimming pools indulge those of us who can afford them – so much easier to be indoors in a heated space rather than chase the sun on a winter's day. Give me the simple pleasures any day!

Kindness

*Life is made up of, not of great sacrifices or duties,
but of little things, in which smiles and kindnesses
and small obligations, given habitually, are what win
and preserve the heart and secure comfort.* Sir Humphry Davy

9th July 2014

I glance out of the bedroom window glad I'm warm inside with no other commitments for the day other than a married couple counselling session. People come and go for counselling from my little unit now. As sometimes happens, they cancel appointments leaving me with a free day. No problem, setting up is easy with light and movable cane furniture lending itself to constant change – I love this casual style of living.

We're often concerned about sudden change or changes upsetting our plans but I'm not concerned at all. Listening to the continuous downpour in the already saturated garden I emulate Pidge holed up somewhere warm and safe, biding his time until the weather allows him to reclaim his domain – there'll be no sitting under the pergola this morning, and no seed.

During the first year on our property, Sundarra, it rained unseasonably, and unreasonably. The table-grape growers lost their livelihood that year. They watched many months of hard work turn into mould and mildew on their precious fruit, saved what they could, and sold the damaged crops to winemakers at ridiculous prices. Then came a widespread drought which ravished country Victoria. People were devastated and I learnt what a city dweller would never know unless they lived in a rural environment, how the weather can destroy one's livelihood. I panicked when it rained on yoga-teaching days. The loamy clay track leading to the main road into town, though built slightly above the flood plain which the land mostly consisted of, became impassable.

Incapable of manoeuvring a vehicle on the two-kilometre track, our only connection to the world, there was no way the main highway was reachable. Right from the start, as beautiful as the property was, I suspected it wasn't going to be easy living! I needed to *toughen up* in a way I never had before. One very wet day my husband encouraged me to drive through the soggy track while he sat beside guiding me in my Camry sedan. It was quite an art, firstly to harness my feelings and then to master the driving techniques needed on this slippery, slimy stretch of earth.

The idea was to drive slowly through flat parts of the track, then, when the water-filled pot holes came up, to drive at an angle more quickly, remembering to slow down without braking and align the steering wheel to the middle of the track. If the car threatened to veer off there were to be no sudden moves, just a slow calculated re-direction to the centre. I can't remember how many times my driving skills were tested during the last wet winter on that pesky track before the drought hit. I was ecstatic when we'd accumulated enough money to refurbish it with crushed rock. We'd organised the local rock, sand and heavy machinery guy to fix up the more troublesome sections. We couldn't afford the rest.

How was I going to attract clients and yoga students to Sundarra if they couldn't get in? How could I reach the local community and other country towns if I couldn't get out? Turning Sundarra into a yoga and wellness retreat centre seemed an impossible dream. I felt trapped.

The big sunburnt Yugoslav completed the last section of repair with crushed rock to our hapless track, the section we could afford. Aware that summer would make way for March rains and taunt my driving skills again, I took a few deep breaths and mustering all the courage I could, marched up to this formidable-looking man, casually offered a drink and hung around to make seemingly light conversation. How long had he been in the business, when did he emigrate, and so on? Then I slipped in, *how much would it cost to put crushed rock on the rest of the track? Just a ballpark figure?* Feeling a touch braver after he answered I swallowed and asked the vital question. *Would you complete the rest of the track now, letting us pay it off a little bit at a time, say, $100 per month?*

Sure, why not? He said in his heavy accent.

I was to discover this gruff somewhat abrupt man had a heart of gold. He'd been the sole builder of tracks and roads for local farms, supplying heavy machinery, carting water supplies in times of drought and *saving the day* for many in the district for years. He died three years after I returned to Adelaide. The whole town of Robinvale turned out for the funeral on the day I was making a return visit unaware it had taken place.

Sometimes we forget that it's not just one person or one situation, or event, that helps fulfil our dreams. There are many cogs in the wheel connecting to the source, just as the strands of a spider web draw into the centre, in the place where completion ends. Drought would bring many more challenges to the Mallee. A time when growers couldn't grow anything, water restrictions hitting everyone and especially damaging to farmers of properties with few water rights and no mains water for households. That all-resourceful man could be seen on many a track carting water in his truck to replenish tank supplies where needed. For me the crushed rock he'd laid on the track at instalment rates meant that visitors to the property could easily come and go. The ease of travelling in and out, regardless of weather conditions, encouraged me to introduce yoga, counselling and wellness workshops further afield to places like Nyah, Swan Hill, and even Balranald just over the border.

Drought broke two years after we'd left the property. The ominous day we left Sundarra belied the fact that the worst of the drought was still to hit. Further water restrictions came later – some farms only permitted to pump 25% of their water entitlements from the Murray River. My heart was in a cage when the moving van slithered up the track. A sudden and unexpected downpour had begun early morning and continued into the next day as the last of our belongings were flung into this metal monster scheduled for the docks of Port Melbourne and across the sea to Tasmania. The land I'd come to love cried bitterly while my heart in its sturdy cage could not. Two years earlier dry summer winds had pounded our track blowing much of the sand and loose crushed rock off, leaving sections of it almost bare and unpassable when it rained.

On arrival the moving van got bogged. Eventually, with help from my husband, his trusty Ute and wooden pylons (discarded by electricity linesmen) it managed the last few metres to our back door. The contents of our large homestead weighed the truck down until sodden and earth-bound. It wasn't going anywhere! Overnight the rain gave its final all and the van became even more embedded. It took several hours to free it, with the help of a tractor this time. Finally, at nightfall I watched it slide through the slush of our main track. Like a dark giant monster, it lumbered and slithered all the way to the farm gate at the highway.

I felt desolate and detached – Sundarra did not want to let me go. I turned away from the expansive window of my yoga room – its main purpose to capture the changing beauty of the daily landscape, not this. The emptiness of the house slapped me in the face and plunged heavily inside me.

Comfort

Comfort, like the golden sun,
dispels the sullen shade with her sweet influence
and cheers the melancholy house of care. Rowe

10th July 2014

Storms pass, calm and light follow. The heart cannot remain closed in the face of beauty. The night was tormented by lashings of rain flung onto my bedroom window, unusual in itself since this window is in a corner of my unit protected by the frangipani tree. The endless discordant raindrops on the pergola's plastic roof, a recent addition, demanded my attention constantly.

The Pidge hasn't emerged for days, nor have I, staying inside the comfort of my snug home, busying myself with endless little tasks. My greatest pleasure this winter has been to listen to the rain from the comfort of my warm living room, made cosier by a tiny but effective and economical gas heater. My yoga master teacher said that in life it is wise not to be too comfortable. I take this with a pinch of salt!

Yesterday, apparently, was the coldest day in Adelaide for decades – snow had fallen in some suburbs. I wondered, awakened by the thrashing of the jacaranda in the squall of the night, whether I'd see a layer of snow in the morning. I'd experienced snow, many times before my sixth birthday, it was a part of my life until we migrated to Australia. A glance through the glassed kitchen door as I get my morning cuppa confirms the storm is over. The garden gleaming an iridescent green unlike any I've seen in Australia, more like the green of the European continent.

Being *comfortable* is somewhat of an illusion. After endless activity, periods of creating, planning and doing I invariably need to indulge in reflective stillness. Being *comfortable* is good for me, providing I don't spend too long doing it! Like now, sitting with my second cup of chai tea, musing on the day ahead and life in general in a warm bed. It's been about three weeks since my fall and find it awkward to sit cross-legged for meditation. Instead, after a cuppa or two, I light the *diva* (butter lamp) and meditate in the cosiness of my bed. It was a silly fall. I'd just completed a two-hour counselling session and stood from the chair only to find, too late, my right foot had fallen asleep and couldn't take the weight of my body. I fell, much to the concern of my clients, crumpling gracefully onto the floor in a state of surprise – the physical feeling non-existent, until much later. The foot, heavily bruised up past the ankle, required some R & R but remarkably, nothing was broken.

Finally, relinquishing the comfort of my bed I get on with another day in semi-retirement; free to restructure my day in tune with my personal agendas and whims as they arise. The feeling of *what am I going to do with the rest of my life* slowly abates as I plan for three regular yoga classes – one in the evening in a nearby hall and the other two in my spacious unit.

The Present
He who neglects the present throws away all he has. Schiller

2nd September, 2014

Suddenly it's spring. Rest and recuperation, together with regular clients and classes conducted from the comfort of my home have replaced my writing rituals. The quiet day meanders nicely while a sense of fulfilment grows within me as I prepare for tomorrow's lunch for a healthy living workshop. A part of me urging me into hurry mode has succumbed to the pull of this lazy afternoon. Soft breezes usher leaves fallen from trees along the gully, the natural border of my garden, on a day where activity and reflection go hand in hand. Recent busyness has taken me away from the Pidge who suddenly lands near the water bowl and is very present. He struts around inspecting territory and glances in my direction nudging me for his seed, as always with an air of patience bordering on impatience – being present but anticipating the future.

This uplifting week is an *afterward* of the mindful immersion of last week's yoga teacher- training course, four days of supporting would-be yoga teachers. When I'm teaching I'm only a small part in the process of a larger whole without which life would be barren. Just the simple pleasure of sitting here, yes, under my pergola, brings me to fully experience the flow of life.

The time spent, and rewards gathered, from yoga support roles, and through teaching classes provide *proof of life* – connection with others fuelled by reflective moments makes living more meaningful. Immersion in the world of yoga enables us to be who we really are; we are accepted. It's almost as if, in any involvement with yoga I'm held in an endless loving embrace where the past doesn't matter, only the present in each precious moment. The many years of teaching and mentoring haven't made me a master but rather reminded me that I'm on a continuous cycle of learning. This awareness hasn't come instantly, but manifested gradually over many courses and classes wherein by supporting others, I'm given so much in return. It is in quiet moments that the wisdom of what I've taught comes alive, dropping into me even deeper than before – it's as if when I teach, I learn.

I recall a session where a student, a self-employed event coordinator, related her experiences of daily yoga practice. Nothing had changed in her life; her job and family circumstances were the same. What had changed was her capacity to live more in tune with the nuances of life and her confidence in asking for help. The nature of her work compelled her to depend on herself – invited to a training seminar and asked to bring a support person with her, she was at a loss. How could she do this, she worked alone? Then suddenly she realised that her business was successful because she already *had* all the support needed – from her loving husband. In an opportunity that may have been so easily missed, the husband, her *support person* of many years, went to the seminar with her. Our mentors are often under our noses; we just need to ask for help and invite them into our lives!

Within me sits an easiness of *being here now*. It's as if I belong nowhere, I am in no time. I just arrive, dependent on no recognition and no-one. I've become an expert in foraging, when I need resources, just like the pigeon, I invite them in!

Silence

Silence is the element in which great things fashion themselves together, that, at length, they may emerge, full-formed and majestic, into the daylight of life. Carlyle

7th September 2014

Sometimes significant changes arrive in our lives in small ways. Our unspoken yearnings for things to be one way or another begin to take form. Over the last twenty years, what has happened, planned and unplanned, required me to engage in things I'd normally not consider without much contemplation.

I've been sitting under my pergola for several hours rugged up from the cold, with cotton wool in my ears in a silent world where sounds are muted or non-existent. I'm in a bubble where the only prolonged and regular sound is the beating of my heart. The *ambos* who came in response to my cry of help last Wednesday gave me a complete medical assessment and gleefully told me I had a strong and healthy heart. This was not news to me since I'd, unavoidably, listened to its steady beat for four days.

A very severe inner ear infection the doctor had said a few days before that, *never seen quite like it in an adult*. The *ambos* responded when, despite the doctor's medication, the centre of my inner ear became an exploding volcano. I found myself in a spinning room, hot, clammy and disoriented – the heart literally jumping out of my chest at the thought that my hearing loss may be permanent. Today, on my second more potent dose of antibiotics, I make a conscious decision to dismiss the thought and allow things to run their course.

A surreal existence has taken hold of me as I try to centre myself calmly in each moment, resting, comforted by books of remarkable accounts of people's extraordinary lives which rescue me from mine. I've read three of these in less than a week. Back outside I watch a persuasive breeze encourage the branches of the jacaranda into movement then flow through the bamboo and palms beyond the back fence into the neighbouring treed environment. I sense, rather than hear, this spectacle of nature in my soundless world, the air warm, gentle on my face ensconced in the scarf protecting my ears. My heartbeat, as if a loud ticking clock is pressed against each ear, is the only sound I hear. It should be disconcerting, but it's not!

During the week I've slept long hours, solidly and more soundly than I ever remember sleeping. *Soundly,* what an ironic way to describe a good sleep! Compelled to change from *doer* to full-time observer, I've discovered there is much value to be found in a soundless world. It is frightening, comforting and illuminating. At night the rhythm and sound of the heartbeat lulls me into deep sleep. Enthralled by its power, I finally understand why the heart focus meditation technique I've practised and taught for years is one of the most restful and profound. Undoubtedly because it is the first sound heard in the mother's womb, its soothing rhythm providing comfort and love. I marvel at the healing power of the body; when the infection was at its most potent and my hearing diminished, the heartbeat became more audible than I'd ever experienced.

At first, I found this alarming, thinking another sinister condition, like tinnitus, was taking hold. Years earlier, a client I'd been seeing regularly for stress management developed tinnitus after major surgery, so severe he'd been unable to sleep for weeks before he sought my help. A mind/body concentration exercise on a continuous reel audio cassette to use at night worked for him. I'm now wondering if listening to his heartbeat would have worked just as well.

Over the last few days, the heart rhythm has drawn me to childhood memories. In my early years my parents often had disagreements, sometimes continuing long after I was put to bed. Those years were riddled with visits to the doctor for ear infections. And now this! I ask myself, *is there something I don't want to hear*? Life is good, isn't it?! My eldest son has given me the most amazingly beautiful grandchildren. I can't help but think that children come into our lives as gifts, given for a short time and I need to be mindful about what I say. Anything spoken in their presence should be warm, loving and encouraging so in moving on to adulthood they take the words with them.

Trust
That, in tracing the shade, I shall find out the sun… Lord Lytton

September 2014

I'm not sure of today's date, I only know I'm into the third week of recovery. A couple of weeks ago the ear nose and throat specialist thoroughly examined my ears and after an audio check said my condition had contributed to temporary deafness. In a medical procedure the next day, he inserted grommets into the swollen ear canals which had completely closed up. Faint sounds began to return, as if I'd walked from a silent room to another which was noise-filled.

Three days on I'm listening to birds again, the wind in trees and even television programmes, muted but listenable, thank goodness for subtitles. The sound of the cooing Pidge soothing my heart and my ears draw my attention to his endearing qualities. Patience and trust remain constant despite conflicts with feathered or human folk, or when the desired seeds fail to appear, reminding me to be tolerant and trusting of the healing process.

As I heal, the outside the world goes on but does not tempt me; I seem to have lost interest in it. I don't owe it anything nor does it *owe* me. It's as if I'm on an island, remote, beautiful and happy to be here, listening, relishing the sense of hearing which in my lifetime I've mostly ignored. My first experience of an island, apart from Grado, my birthplace, was Kangaroo Island, little knowing at the time that years on I'd live there. The visit in early 1980's was on a holiday with my first husband; we'd taken a few days off from the boys leaving them with grandparents. My first flight in a tiny plane with propellers unlocked the extrovert in me who rarely ventured beyond a perfectly composed exterior. Sitting immediately behind the pilot I literally had a birds' eye-view of the world. Aware I was craning my neck to get a good look through window he invited me to sit by him as we came in sight of the island – the jewel in a sapphire sea took my breath away.

The expansive screen not only opened up to the view in front of me but to my whole world, making it small and manageable, a *birds-eye* view of life. Suddenly it was full of possibility beyond the marriage and motherhood encapsulating my life and designing the me I was becoming. I played my roles perfectly, unaware of any disconnection from the rest of the world, unaware of an exciting life passing me by. I lived the life everyone in my shoes seemed to lead while the inside me remained untouched. This wonderous vision of the island awakened me from the self-imposed sleep of duty and responsibility taking over who I really was. Marriage and motherhood had given me *status*. I fitted into the world exemplified by my parents, parents-in-law and all the extended families, friends and other mothers, cocooned in a place preventing another view of the world.

The airplane's gentle glide over Kangaroo Island on that picture-perfect day lifted me out of the *raincoat syndrome* I'd been experiencing where nothing much touched me. I could see life and its happenings but nothing really penetrated very deeply. For the rest of our holiday on the Island I donned my raincoat again. We stayed in American River in-between coach tours of the Island which didn't quite have the effect of that first bird's eye view of the Island. American River though uniquely beautiful, for some unknown reason didn't ignite a spark leaving me with a strangely depressed feeling. Thirty years on, revisiting as a yoga teacher, that same feeling returned like an all-pervading grief that had nothing to do with the present. Maybe it's whaling history and the Aboriginal women caught in it had left its mark on this beautiful place. Now, more aware of myself and my connection with the world, when I find myself inadvertently wearing my old raincoat I remove it, trusting that whatever the experience, *good* or *bad*, I'm in control.

Action
Our actions are our own; their consequences belong to heaven. Francis

1st December 2014

A shying away from what has given a measure of satisfaction threatens me. It's been over two months since I've written anything and I resist what came easily and naturally. The illness just passed has interrupted established routines and unsettled me. The germ aggressive in its intent to invade my body, though diminished, has invaded my life. I don't want to think about it, or indeed write about it, as I return slowly to routines, tending the garden and addressing the ever-present demanding Pidge.

However, I can't block a lurking sense of fulfilment as I approach Christmas; not so much from work completed but from resolves and desires dealt with. Transition from full-time work to semi-retirement is over. Forced to let go of past routines, after all that's what they were, and accept this new stage of my life, a truce has evolved. I shake hands with a new way of living, more leisure time – no, not *leisure*, different ways of doing things and more time to do them in.

The grapevine's new leaves stretch along the pergola railings to create a delicate viewing window to the garden. Birds continue to visit the small water bowl placed strategically for encouragement between bushy plants. Camaraderie is developing slowly. Visiting birds and creatures edge away respectfully from the pigeons and others they're not acquainted with at the water bowl. Last week I glanced up from my notebook delighted by one of the resident lizards, paws in water, taking long luxurious sips, mostly ignored by Pidge scratching for lost seed and the piping shrike swaggering around waiting his turn.

I spend early mornings sitting under the pergola with new purpose, to immerse in nature's stillness, replenish and strengthen my resolve to go out into my other world. The last three evenly-paced weeks allowed me to travel to full recovery. The senior yoga teacher-training tutors are in town requiring my support again, admin work and preparations for a national yoga conference. Sourcing venues and flower-arranging have become my roles, pleasant enough tasks but, ironically, flowers are a devastatingly destructive force for my sinuses.

Pidge inspects his domain with swift glances toward me, no doubt expecting more seed! I'm not sure how many birds have landed in the limited space around the water bowl, but invariably he struts around it with a measure of patience then closes in until his huffiness prompts them to leave. Meanwhile, on the other side of the garden the sprinkler is on, the latest visitors, the tiniest of birds, finches I think, fly through the misty stream with unbridled joy. They swoop into the soft, steady soda spray and dart into the lavender bush close to my viewing platform unafraid, or unaware, of my presence behind the vine. Tiny silver eyes beam from the greyish plumage tinted with a film of green glimpsed only in sunlight. Petite wings flap with pleasure as they dart back to the water then trail into the pink holly hock, the lavender plant and back to the sprinkler again – swooping, circling and relishing a secret game.

We invariably make independent, unprovoked decisions and actions with little prodding or cajoling, yet, whether planned or unplanned, every action brings reaction. Having watered this little patch of lawn last night without conscious thought, I'm amazed at the number of birds it's attracted this morning. Rewarded by their antics I turn on the sprinkler again – we're influenced by everyone and everything, whether aware of it or not.

Looking up from scribblings I see another of the resident lizards, there are two I think, as it edges perfectly camouflaged from the bushy side of the garden to the water bowl. He drinks daintily, little pointy paws over the rim of the bowl, with great relish and satisfaction ignoring a black and white piping shrike watching with great curiosity. New flocks of birds, arriving shyly at first, converge into the garden to join family groups enjoying the ambience, aware of my presence but taking little notice.

The *play of God* continues in this little piece of nature. Three pigeons vie for lost seed in moist blades of grass until the piping shrikes confront them with pushy bravado. But the Pidge, with puffed out breast holds his own, resigned to the strangers' presence, struts and huffs until he claims the water bowl for the rest of his flock.

Gratitude
A thankful heart is not only the greatest virtue,
but the parent of all the other virtues. Cicero

8th December 2014

The positive side of life is a much better place to live in! Yesterday morning I thumbed through old notebooks with scrawls of writings as far back as 1994. The nineties were complex, full of change and adversity; these days I'd describe it as *challenging*. Fortunately, I've come to understand that every day is *a good day*, only our perception of what happens in it can make it *a bad day*.

Days are just days, the sun rising and setting regardless of daily living and weather patterns. Weather is just weather, in whatever season. Right? Wrong! If the moon controls tides, then, presumably, it has the power to disturb the body's water tables too. In medieval times dances were performed to encourage and celebrate harvests – did they make a difference? Yes! Not necessarily directly to the harvest but the way it drew people together to cultivate for successful harvests, immersing them with nature and each other, if nothing else. Few have time to sit, ponder and watch their garden grow and view the flurry of its daily visitors. I'm lucky, or perhaps I'm making a conscious choice to be lucky and be grateful for all I have.

The family of piping shrikes, spindly legs jerking across the lawn foraging for titbits, feed my soul. Watching this tiny display of nature fills me with gratitude and is my way of celebrating it. Drawn to observe nature, even in *bad* times, reflective stillness brings balance into my day, regardless of any *good* or *bad* events in them.

A pensive child, observation from an early age has imbued me with remarkable memory. Incredibly, I still recall events from my earliest childhood. The day my younger brother was born is crystallised in memory. My older brother and I, warm in the cosy kitchen of an upstairs apartment in a small country town called Aurisina, waited for his arrival. It was here, nestled in the hilly parts of northern Italy and the then Yugoslavian border, Papacci had settled his young family close to his posting in the *Polizia Venezia Giulia*. The police force, formed just after the Second World War by the allies, was a response to the turbulent aftermath of changed conditions in border regions. The Italian Carabinieri would have struggled for acceptance within the narrow margins of land where Yugoslavs and Italians, living there for decades, suddenly found themselves residing *on the wrong side of the fence.* When governments re-established the borders some people discovered unexpectedly they were no longer in native territory, either Italian or Yugoslavian.

On a snowy Christmas Eve my youngest brother was born. Papacci strode into the tiny kitchen, tall and presiding in his dark winter coat flecked with wisps of snow, a thick woollen scarf drawn around his neck up to his ears, with the midwife – a formidable-looking darkhaired woman carrying a large brown leather bag. He came over to the two of us huddled in a corner and in a large embrace said, *stay here now, and you'll soon see the new baby.* In my most assertive little girl voice I reminded him that I'd been promised a baby sister and excitedly asked, *where is she?* He pointed hurriedly to the midwife's large bag and said, *Si, Si! The baby's in there.* And with that, accompanied this strange woman through a door of the kitchen and into the bedroom where Mammina was ready to birth in the traditional way.

Later, dwarfed at the foot of a very large steel-frame bed, I peered at Mammina holding a tiny blanketed thing, barely recognisable as a baby. Papacci's firm hand on my back urged me forward, *Go, go up and give your new brother a kiss.* A brother?! No, he was obviously mistaken, *you said I could have a baby sister,* I responded tearfully. It was *not* a good day, even though it was for everyone else.

In Aurisina I was regularly on the receiving end of copious amounts of sugared water, when Mammina left to *far la spesa* (go shopping), administered by the capable hands of five-year older brother put in charge. Leaving him with strict instructions to look after me I sat on blanketed kitchen floor surrounded by a paraphernalia of wooden spoons, pots and pans. When I exhausted the *toys* on the blanket and became restless, he'd take it upon himself to concoct a mixture of sugared water and feed it to me with a teaspoon.

Not wanting to leave me and the baby alone, occasionally Mammina would send him on errands in the multi-storied apartment building with a cup and instructions to *go downstairs to la signora, and ask if you can borrow, 'per piacere'* (please), *a cup of semolina – tell her I'll pay her back tomorrow.* Semolina was my favourite breakfast cereal; I couldn't quite take to the *pane e caffe* (bread and coffee) my brother loved.

Death
Death is the liberator of him whom freedom cannot release,
the physician of whom medicine cannot cure, and
the comforter of him whom time cannot console. Colton

10th December 2014

The writing in my head is more superior than what lands on the page in front of me. The simple act of putting pen to paper prompts the left-brain to order and sequence words into readable chunks, unlike thoughts landing gracefully and effortlessly like butterflies. This morning, my mind, like the weather drifts with soft eloquence from the present to the past, then back again and tiptoes into the future.

A mellow, sunless day with the dewy moistness of overnight earth flavouring the atmosphere hints at rain, calming the day before it begins. I'm inspired by the simplicity of life in these calm reflective moments guiding me to contemplation. It's been ten years since Papacci died. I recall it as a poignantly tender funeral, left for me to organise. My older brother gave me snippets to include in the eulogy, little things I'd forgotten. Days earlier I wasn't sure whether the funeral would go ahead. The drama I'd been plunged into at a major South Australian hospital, resulting in being accompanied by police officers to *view the body*, left me in a daze. I kept it from the rest of the family, quietly grieving in their own way. I constantly had to remind myself that Papacci's celebration of his life was all that mattered and wouldn't allow my emotions, or anything else, get in the way.

Papacci's indomitable will, finesse and appreciation of public display and performance, encapsulated in the Italian phrase *far figura*, rescued me. The final event of his life needed to reflect this. My brain so scrambled with all the last-minute preparations, I didn't write the eulogy

Until the day of the funeral; after another sleepless night I sat up in bed as tears and writing flowed onto the page. What evolved was a celebration he'd have been proud of. A beautiful Sudanese woman, his carer for the preceding three months before his final stint in hospital, was part of this.

Discussing his funeral around the dining table, the family learnt she'd had a lengthy conversation with him in hospital the week before he died. She told us he was lucid, charming and joyful. Papacci at his best! She had brought out these qualities with remarkable ease. He'd confided to her that he was *ready to go* but afraid of what would happen to the family if he *let go of the reins*. It was because of her brief but intimate connection with Papacci we included her in the funeral celebrations. It isn't how long you know a person that matters, but how deep the connection is to make them *family*.

The local parish priest, face lined with a map of his life, informed us, clearly not wanting to prolong the ceremony with *unnecessary embellishments,* that ours would be the first of two funerals that afternoon. I held his gaze and said with great emphasis *my father's final celebration of his life and death is not to be compromised* and detailed what I'd planned. A display to be set up in front of his coffin representing his life would include family photographs, his mandolin, the hymn books from which he conducted the Italian church choir and a large peace candle from which others would be lit and passed around to family and friends. In the last few months of his life it sat on the dresser in the hall of my parents' home along with photos of deceased family members and an array of religious icons. His carer, a talented musician and entertainer, would do a celebratory presentation around his coffin.

Papacci's funeral became the celebration he deserved. She sang with great feeling and earthy tones a song she'd composed bearing his name. I couldn't help but see a mental image of Papacci sitting on his coffin clapping his hands and shouting, *Brava! Brava!* Finally, flicking her blue shawl from her shoulders and over her head, she sang the Ave Maria in Swahili – the Ave Maria I'd learnt at school as a young migrant, albeit in English. We were all visibly moved for more reasons than I can imagine.

I tried to keep the eulogy short, highlighting things he'd shared with me throughout his life. Like the time he'd chuckled over his first *Learn to speak English class* aboard the ship on the migratory journey to Australia. The teacher, gesturing animatedly, had pointed to a passing ship saying *look, look,* until the class peered through the port holes to *look.* Days later it dawned on him that a ship was not called '*look*'. His talents and qualities surpassed only by his family loyalty and profound sense of justice emanating from a large heart were worthy of celebration!

Two sons and three adult grandchildren carried his coffin to the strains of the *Alleluia Chorus* regularly included in his Sunday choir programmes. I grieved little after that, my grieving happened when he was alive. The suffering and deprivation he'd experienced in childhood during the First World War and subsequent Depression were thinly disguised throughout his life, as were the after-effects of his military service in the Second World War of which he would rarely speak.

Beginnings
*Begin whatever you have to do:
the beginning of a work stands for the whole.* Ausonius

29th December 2014

Little has changed – the pigeons still chase each other around the garden to re-establish their pecking order. What *has* changed is the piping shrike's behaviour; he drinks at the water bowl, glancing up now and again seemingly bemused by their antics – pushiness a thing of the past.

Can we change our behaviours and make successful new beginnings? Can we re-start our lives and move on from the old with renewed energy, commitment and an inspiring sense of purpose? I think so, providing we aren't precious about holding onto past happenings, people and things!

As I transition from 2014 to the new year, I embrace the opportunity to create something different, vibrant and sustaining. The ending of the old year and beginning of a new one is not just a modern way of enticing us into celebrations of social and economic importance. We celebrate birthdays don't we!? Why not use the end of the twelfth month to acknowledge and release what has been and move unencumbered into the future? After all, isn't the frantic lead-in to Christmas a death throe, a final fluttering of a wounded bird before it succumbs to stillness!?

The lull of Christmas afterward greets me on the back pergola. The neighbours either side of my unit have ceased all activity, celebratory noise disappeared into a natural void. The invisible woman with the strident voice behind the raggedy plank fence at the bottom of the garden has settled. Her grating, rasping smoker's cough non-existent. *Where has she gone? Back to rehab?* Respite from the pungent fumes of hash and tobacco and her frequent visitor with the croaky accented voice is a balm to my soul.

I relish this quiet day of wispy cool summer breezes and reflect on the year – another gone in a *woosh*. Yesterday a group of yogis gathered here for a celebration of peace. We come together regularly for this peace meeting; a lovely sharing from the deepest part of our hearts, a time to pray and chant in Sanscrit, an ancient time-honoured language, with great reverence for all 2014 has given and to welcome in the new. With common purpose and open hearts, it's easy to forgive and let go of what has happened to better embrace another beginning.

Boldness
Fortune befriends the bold. Dryden

25th January 2015

The Pidge knows no fear. Pigeons may look the same but what sets Pidge apart is his fearless attitude. He sits on the fence and cocks his head at me, the signal for me to get up and provide him with seed. I know it's him and not any other old pigeon, the only one standing his ground when I sprinkle seed around the water bowl while others roost in the jacaranda, waiting expectantly. He doesn't approach too closely until I sit in my usual spot under the pergola with my ritualistic toast and cuppa. He's the leader, the others clearly followers. When he begins to peck a flock of feathered friends join him for the feed – he *has* been busy this spring!

In-between pecks he admonishes one, then another, re-asserting his territory with brazen boldness. Though they put up a good fight he ultimately wins. However, another unexpected challenge meets him head on – piping shrike numbers have increased too. Pidge ignores the leader until, with a few shrill calls, his opponent enlists help. Soon the pigeons are surrounded by the rest of the shrike family. Challenging indeed, even for a brave pigeon! It's bad enough having your own family vying for control, but now this! Pidge continues to hold firm when frenetic antics follow even though family members desert him.

Establishing myself as a yoga teacher in country Victoria was a bit like the pigeon scenario. Naively I thought of myself as the *Lone Ranger* taking yoga into unchartered territory. *Easy,* I would introduce yoga in my local town, Robinvale, only seventeen kilometres away, with a few flyers and ads in the local *rag*. There was no yoga teacher in the district. Good! And a church hall next to the school. Good! I pictured a throng of eager parents attending classes if I carefully slotted in the time when the kids were dropped off at school. Wrong!

Despite the parish priest's keenness for me to use the church hall for yoga classes, my use of the space was short-lived. In preparation I'd spent many hours cleaning floors under his watchful eye encouraging me with, *you're doing a sterling job.* The nice quiet thin man with rivulets of grey through thin slicked-down straight hair, prised open the stubborn sash windows, which he explained had been painted shut at the last working bee.

No throngs clamouring to do yoga entered the spotless hall, less than a handful. Only two faithfully remained when I relocated to the Robinvale Aged Care facility where I volunteered. Classes were slow there too, people dipping their toes in for one or two classes then disappearing. Rather than an interest in yoga, it was a *come and see* what the new girl in town was about. Having only just completed my second diploma of yoga training in my fifties my confidence took a slide as I slowly came to terms with the fact that teaching yoga is secondary to learning how to fit in and live in a small country town.

Despite losing a degree of confidence, the *Taurus* in me didn't give up. I decided to take yoga into other country towns with some success.

Fairies

Wherever is love and loyalty, great purposes and lofty souls, even though in a hovel or a mine, there is fairyland. Kingsley

7th February 2015

The fairies at the bottom of the garden are happy! How do I know? My granddaughter tells me so. As she disappears under the jacaranda tree among the leafy undergrowth, now quite prolific with spring-like offerings of tiny violets, the birds are nowhere to be seen.

An imaginative, mostly focused child but at times rambunctious, she clomps with great delight in what we call *the fairy garden.* Fairies, real and imagined, hide between the large leaves of the jacaranda's squat companion, the loquat tree. *Visible* fairies, purchased with great care from garden shops, vie for position under its wide-leafed canopy over the miniature violet garden, sharing space with audacious brightly-coloured gnomes needing a touch-up.

Grandchildren visits have been few over the last couple of months, Christmas and summer school holidays taking them away to grandparents, interstate. The older sibling will join a cricket team this year, his *likes* becoming more refined and focused; at age nine he's become more confident in his sporting ability. I foresee him as a human being with a great purpose in life, a thinker with a penchant to sensitivity, holding his ground alongside peers more interested in the physical attributes of life. The *princess,* on the other hand, tackling bikeriding and climbing formidable playground equipment, is a great encourager and a vigorous sparring partner in all games.

Some time ago, on a day of dense humidity and heat, I shuddered with fatigue at her suggestion of playing *hide and seek* in the garden.

Fortunately, it was a listless day for her too. So, I encouraged her to think about something else she might like to do. *Let's do Christmas together,* she chortled with inspiration. Right, I was ready for this! Old Christmas cards bundled onto a small card table under the pergola together with scissors, glue and coloured *textas*. A small barren Christmas tree, a real one in a pot, waited nearby expectantly. Afternoon tea consumed and over with, we sat among the paraphernalia of bits and pieces waiting to be transformed into decorations. We all *have* to join in, she emphasised.

Her brother, keen to practise his cricket bowling but usually compliant, with a shrug of his shoulders went with the plan. There's no getting out of it when his little sister reasons *you're part of the family and when we come here, we **have to** do family things.* I wonder where that came from?!

Home
*Home should be an oratorio of the memory, singing to all
our afterlife melodies and harmonies of old-remembered joy.* Henry W. Beecher

11th February 2015

The garden, moist and cool with morning waterings, belies the promise of a warm day. The compacted green lawn with masses of greenery on one side of the stepping stones leading to the garden shed emanates coolness while the other side, patchy and dry, recovers from dandelion weeds. The neighbour gave me the name of a product good for annihilating broad-leafed weeds while at the same time fertilising the lawn– so weeks later I hunt for it in a local garden outlet. I'd inadvertently converted its name to *flow and grow* resonating with my tendency to poeticise. The salespeople hadn't heard of it but they *did* have another product with a similar name which they said was very good.

The copious amounts of seed sprinkled near the water bowl remain largely untouched. The piping shrikes strut around it with spindly legs and an air of superiority while a lonely pigeon, not Pidge the bold one, hovers nearby. A pair of black and yellow New Holland honey eaters, making regular visits to the hollyhocks, disappear into the coolness of leafy tree canopies where rosellas contribute stridently to the cacophony of early morning bird calls. Finally, mid-morning, the bird life settles to prepare for the humid heat promised by a fading blue sky.

A number of things in my head demand attention trying to warn me off procrastination but I refuse to listen and continue to write. That feeling of *home,* long absent, is returning. When my youngest son left for his first overseas trip around the world including the United Kingdom to visit friends, a three-month trip his 21st birthday gift, I was in the throes of a second marital separation.

Quietly distraught that among everything else happening in my life, he wouldn't return to the home he'd lived in for the past ten years of his life, I wondered how it would affect him. In his absence it was sold. I moved from the large turn-of-the century villa with the high ceilings and the rambling back yard, where an old almond tree grew among vegetable plots beyond myriads of pot plants and hanging baskets tended by my then partner. Too busy with full-time school teaching and artistic pursuits I left the gardening to him.

My son returned to a small modest art-deco home I'd bought in a less prestigious area. He'd written on the postcard preceding him in his creative, uniquely grandiose way, that he had no inclination to live in *suburbia* and when he returned to live with me, it *wouldn't be for long*. My response was simple: *This is my home and I'm inviting you to share it with me. A home is not just bricks and mortar in a particular place, in a specific suburb – home is a place in your heart you take with you wherever you go.* It was a somewhat prophetic statement. In the following years I set up *home* in different places at least nine times, two in which I was house-sitting.

In this small unit with the surprise garden expanding into the gully where water trickles in winter, I have the luxury of observing my domain and its feathered friends from the comfort of a pergola framed by a flourishing grapevine. Today, however, I find myself pondering life and its lessons with the tiniest bit of disquiet in me, a slight feeling of uneasiness that this beautiful welcoming place where I'm beginning to enjoy retirement, will be temporary too.

Pigeons and shrikes return from their secret roosts and meander around the moist, cool garden. A fearless little honey eater skims over the water bowl, across the feathered groups resuming their pecking at left-over seeds, and then to the lavender bush only an arm- length away. Aware of my presence, she eyes me curiously, possibly wondering if she's disturbed my domain, or perhaps, if I'll disturb hers.

I've allowed others to trespass on my territory many times, giving up personal space to accommodate them, to keep them happy. When it became uncomfortable, I conveniently took myself to work, or should I say overwork, spending too much time absorbed in various projects. In the final year of my time with the one who tended the garden, my immersion in the arts was one of my most prolific and creative eras. It was if I'd acquired the *Midas touch*; my first books were published, radio plays and theatre pursuits all found ground. He'd withdrawn to the world of university study, student sojourns and other get-togethers I wasn't aware of at the time. So, no *World War Three* when we parted, no *us,* only two individuals who'd been *doing their own thing* for a long time.

I gaze fondly at my feathered visitors knowing they take only what they need.

Observation

*He alone is an acute observer who can observe
Minutely without being observed.* Lavatar

18th February, 2015

No matter where I go my mind comes with me, the one where all kinds of memories are stashed. Thankfully, I now direct it to observe rather than introspect too deeply to avoid painful feelings belonging to past events. The daily meditation practice begun in 1995, such a long time ago, apart from infusing me with calm, has undoubtedly influenced my brain. Now in my sixties, I wonder how deeply the practice has influenced the *grey matter* and what my emotional make-up would be if not for this focussed extraordinary practice.

On the lush lawn the pigeons and piping shrikes are not only pecking at seed but vying to establish territorial order, again. The *shrike leader* has a good splash around in the spacious new water bowl I've set above the ground while the pigeons plod around the small one, feeling, like me, safe on the ground. Observing the luscious green of my well-watered patch of earth, I do what I did yesterday – surveying, sampling or choosing to do something with what I'm seeing. I can change my little environment; pull out a weed here, pick a flower there, move a pot plant, prune a bush, crop and alter to suit myself.

Yesterday I had fewer choices – a vegetable sandwich, three choices of bread and the decadence of an iced coffee (without cream) which I dawdled over. I entertained myself by viewing the world beyond my garden and observed humanity drawn into the fascination of the senses. Happily I indulged in a light lunch at a small shopping mall café and watched shoppers of various shapes and forms rush, stroll, meander, glide and circle in a multidirectional dance around me as if I was in a goldfish bowl in a soundless world. A fashion boutique with the usual doorway displays of discounted clothing, cajoled women to browse, enter and buy. In dribs and drabs they examined, fingered or bypassed – so much to choose from!

It had been a long time since I'd sat alone and done this. I do this from time to time with other aspects of life, newspapers, television, a social sojourn. It's almost as if there's an unspoken need to revisit and review my old life and compare it to the new, or maybe, to check if it is still there. My life of stillness, simple pleasures, reflections and self-awareness allows me the indulgence of unhurried choices, adding to my existence in a way that betters my world and my place in it.

Earlier in the week I'd been involved in a bustle of students training to be yoga teachers. As a volunteer support-tutor I easily centre myself in the role, mostly among strangers, feeling no demands, personal energy intact in that part of me that cannot be ruffled, as it was yesterday undisturbed by passers-by. Years of daily meditation practice allows me the benefit of observing how everyone else lives. Instinctively I sense when my centre of stillness becomes affected and return to a place which nourishes me – these days it's my home and garden environment where I'm nourished and any depleted energy restored.

My master yoga teacher said we can evaluate any experience it in terms of energy by simply asking, *Will it give to me, or will it take away?*

Perseverance
Great works are performed not by strength but by perseverance. Johnson

23rd February, 2015

The count is now eleven pigeon regulars pecking at meagre offerings. The seed, not meant to feed them, is a treat. Pidge at first glance is anonymous but becomes recognisable by a flurry of wings if anyone tries to invade his personal space. I recognise him instantly by his habits. When all are gone, he's a stayer continuing to source any remnants lost in the grass. He doesn't disappear at the first sign of difficulty; he was here first, instinct and initiative hand in hand led him here for extra nourishment. He'd tolerate one or two of his flock, the sharing incidental, and shoo the rest away as if they were invaders.

When my two children were in primary school an incidental opportunity beckoned me, school-teaching. Thirteen years later the nourishment dropped away and I moved on. Being selfish is okay especially when trying to replenish with what is by-passed at the dinner table. Over forty or so years ago I found myself debilitated in a first marriage and no longer absorbing the goodness of life. I was living someone else's life. My mother's? Perhaps, but more of an ideal I'd invented, different from hers, in a home I created where *you could eat off the floor.*

As a teenager I was reminded on several different fronts that a woman's place was in the home – keeping it clean and making sure the husband and everyone, was fed, clothed and happy. This may have been Mammina's ideal – a dream not fulfilled since she worked six days a week, the house usually untidy with not enough hours in a day to keep it otherwise. Papacci, often between jobs and despondent because of health conditions, felt kept. I dreamt of a time where I'd be free of all this, a time when I didn't have demands placed on how and when I did household chores. At age eleven, resentful at being allocated piles of ironing to be completed before Mammina arrived home from work, I procrastinated. My mind on more important things, like creating the world I wanted to live in, filled with romance fuelled by music, dancing and writing.

During school holidays the radio became a great companion; music from classical to pop filled the living room while my brothers gallivanted outdoors wherever boys go with mates when parents work. My red felt slippers zipped up snugly around my feet allowed me the poise of a ballerina and I'd tippy-toe around the ironing board to the classical pieces emanating from Radio 5CL. Books and poetry-writing further stimulated my romantic view of the world and, according to Mammina, made me lazy. I would have liked to marry the boy across the road who I had a big crush on and live happily ever after. But I discovered, when I moved on from Enid Blyton to Dickens, that not all books told stories with happy endings.

My first library encounter was in a little corner house in Evandale, across the road from our school friends; a Dutch family with an indeterminate number of children, eleven or twelve, I think. My first novel, Charles Dickens' *The Olde Curiosity Shop* introduced me to the tragic figure of Little Nell and the notion of martyrdom which I related to very well. I devoured books with a torch under my blankets long after everyone had gone to bed and relied on visits to the library, tagging along whenever my older brother visited his Dutch friends. The only girl in an Italian family, I wasn't allowed to go anywhere unless under his direct supervision, which, fortunately, he was rather careless with and served me well in my teen years.

One of the first books I owned was Enid Blyton's book of fairies. When my older brother and I returned home from stints in orphanages, me at Goodwood and he at Largs Bay, deposited there due to Papacci's workplace accident, he won a book voucher in a competition to design a road safety sign. My father with the three of us in tow, visited a city bookshop. I politely told the *bookshop lady* I wanted a book of Annie Oakley. At nine or ten I'd become fascinated by this famous gun-slinging woman at the pictures. Even at that age I knew what I wanted. But the lady politely and firmly suggested the book was not right for me.

Throughout childhood, invariably, adults tried to distract me from *wants* to something more appropriate. From these experiences I developed resilience arising from the resentment of having to comply with others' will. And so, Enid Blyton's book of fairy stories came into my possession. I loved it, and read it over and over, my first journey into a world of magic.

I discovered the State Library when still in primary school, influenced not only by the Dutch family but Papacci, who took me along when he sourced books to improve his knowledge of the English language. I developed a lifetime relationship with libraries and the simple gifts they offered – free books bringing the whole world to me. So much more exciting than doing the pile of ironing Mammina ambitiously left for me to do before she came home from work. I developed a certain resourcefulness – towels were folded and lightly pressed on top creating an illusion of being ironed. Handkerchiefs came next, neatly folded and also ironed at the top of the pile. Mammina was not fooled, at a glance knowing I'd been procrastinating but never quite worked out what, or how, my time was occupied. Or maybe she did – she was young once and had had dreams too. I still avoid ironing.

In 2012, after a short stint on Kangaroo Island, I re-established connection with another library. Returning to my seaside unit with some sticks of furniture, essentials and few books, mainly reference books, emotionally drained by a failed relationship, my mind needed nurturing. Disturbed by the previous eighteen months, my thoughts needed distraction and redirection. The Brighton library where I'd regularly taken my boys at an early age was still there. I entered through the now automated doors and stepped into a world lost in memory; little had changed, apart from computer stations and automated borrowing services. I felt comforted. I emerged with just the right antidote, James Herriott's *All Creatures Great and Small*.

Heartfelt
Home-keeping hearts are happiest. Longfellow

2nd March 2015

In the cool of morning, which the pigeon is resisting squirreled away somewhere in his hidey hole, I welcome the precious balm of autumn and contemplate what has been. Like the amber leaves falling gracefully off the vine, a memory wafts into the space of my heart, the image of an encounter with one of my master yoga teachers.

On a 2004 retreat at a yoga centre nestled in the valley of Snowdonia I wandered with a small group with soft footsteps into the green and gold of autumn. The Welsh countryside, vibrantly green, accompanied by symphonies of softly flowing streams and tiny waterfalls cascading from miniature embankments, enthralled me. At a clearing a crystal-clear pool invited many feet to plunge into the coolness of rushing water. With much delight two in our group discarded outer clothing and immersed themselves wholly.

Higher up on an embankment I sat ensconced in the trunk of a tree, hollowed over time and covered in moss, wondering why I couldn't indulge with the same kind of abandonment. Instead, I turned to my constant companion, my notebook, and wrote about being embraced by the tree as if safe and protected in a mother's womb. Later, gathered in the yoga hall to celebrate our time together and share personal highlights of our experiences over the last few days, some read from journal reflections. I remembered the poem written in the heart of the tree. After the final sharing I stood bravely and timidly asked permission to race to my room across the hall for my notebook. The teacher nodded but asked me to be quick. I returned and she motioned for me to sit on the dais beside her. I read. The first few words brought an explosion of tears as her calming hand rested gently on my back at heart level and waited patiently for me to gather myself together. The healing arising from that simple gesture stayed with me over the following days until I returned home, and to this day, she has a place in my heart.

Endurance
The bird that flutters least is longest on the wing. Cowper

13th April 2015

It's been some time since Pidge first landed in the garden. His family has grown to modest proportions, the entourage of hangers-on still quibble for small offerings but his feistiness and determination to be the last pigeon standing has remained intact.

Mammina, insisting I stay overnight on one of many trips from Sundarra, my then home in country Victoria, gave me her bed to sleep in and wouldn't take *no* for an answer. On the first overnight stay I lay awake listening to her snoring, shifting and groaning as she slept uncomfortably on the floor in a make-shift lounge bed. Usually, I'd sleep at my son's home on the other side of town but this was no longer practical with Papacci becoming more dependent on her time. I wanted to help. She did everything, cleaned, washed and cooked as well as looked after his personal care. Fine, she was used to it, but in his later years and her senior by ten years, she also became his *gofer*. The TV room was at the far end of the hall and furthest from the kitchen where Mammina busied herself with endless tasks of food preparation, snacks on-call ensuring endless hours of walking exercise. When his tenor voice echoed down the hall of the high-ceilinged villa, *Maria, bring me a drink* or *un pezzetino di formaggio con un biscotto* (a piece of cheese with a biscuit) or, *qualcosa dolce* (something sweet), she'd roll her eyes!

In the final year of his life, I was slight relief on the weekends I came to stay. Mostly I'd aim to relieve her of chores she'd doggedly not want to release. Apart from being the *gofer* she'd become his only companion. The dilemma, she could not split herself in two. I quickly came to understand the problem of being in two places at once; should I take over the cooking or succumb to his request for me to sit with him to *far compagnia* (keep him company)? At times I'd sit guiltily beside him listening to his stories, watching his favourite movies while feeling the need to keep Mammina company and give *her* the practical and emotional support she so needed. Like the Pidge, Mammina was the last one standing, feisty to the end but in terms of generosity poles apart.

It was a battle, as with everything else, to convince her another solution to sleeping arrangements had to be found. She agreed to an alternative when my bottom line was an offer she couldn't refuse, *I won't stay overnight when I return.* Eventually, in the last six months of my visits, the laundry/utility room, infinitely more spacious than most modern bedrooms, became my sleeping quarters.

Mammina and younger brother converted it into a homely bedroom. A steel-framed bed set up on a carpet square on the concrete floor, a sturdy old wooden chair graced with a doily on which sat a lamp became my bedside cabinet and a wooden trunk, the grey paint scratched and worn on our migratory journey from Italy in the fifties, swathed in a floral cloth and adorned with faux flowers, was my dressing table. A heater for cool nights and a laundry clothes rack to hang my clothes completed the picture. I was deeply touched, especially with the flowers and framed pictures of Christian saints telling me this had been Mammina's little project since my last visit.

In 2003, the last year of Papacci's life, I came monthly to cook or sit with him to give Mammina some respite from his ever-increasing needs, or insist that *she* sit while I focussed on kitchen duties. This didn't work out the way I liked! Papacci would insist, always prone to logical arguments, that since I was a visitor I should be the one to *far compagnia* (keep him company). Clever negotiations were needed to give my parents what they needed most!

Change
To the mind, which is itself, no changes bring surprise. Byron

30th April 2015

The comfort of this small garden is beyond measure, a haven for a life slowing into what appears to be an unusual semi-retirement. The sun shines softly through the bamboo slats of what used to be my bed; upended and positioned against the northern side of the pergola it has become a screen and decorative plant holder – a work in progress in terms of hanging pots. The grapevine rustling in the faint morning breeze and boasting colours of gold, orange and brown ushers in the second month of autumn.

Pidge visits with his offspring who are often on the receiving end of random territorial attacks if they try to take over the pecking order. Female friends huff away hoping to discourage the males of the species, ignoring any amorous leanings knowing winter is around the corner and nesting would be out of the question. Rain has hovered over the last few days but only delivered a few spots and though still mildly warm birds visit the water bowl infrequently.

My evening yoga class remains unchanged having no bearing whatsoever on the season. Whether it's hot or cold most students are regulars and keep coming benefiting and enjoying whatever I program into the class; if it were not for their presence, my life wouldn't be as rich. It's as if teaching is a gift bestowed on me long ago in a time beyond recall, another life? A semi-retired night school English teacher who I'd kept in touch with, told me when I was in the throes of completing school-teacher training, that teaching is not something you learn. And she was right *How to teach* wasn't a subject covered in the course. Over time I become aware of what she meant and believed it. Somehow, what comes out of my heart, judging from some students' reaction, lands in theirs. All I know is that sincerity makes its mark without a bow and arrow to guide it.

When I teach yoga, every sense is drawn into each moment, nothing exists but what is happening in front of me. My school-teaching days were like that, not in quite the same sacred way as teaching yoga and meditation, but nonetheless engaging, absorbing and fulfilling. In the three years of teaching at one of my favourite schools near the beach I felt part of a large family. The school population, small for a suburban school, was threatened with if we couldn't attract more children.

Amazingly, twenty-two years on, my new young next-door neighbour tells me she teaches in the very same school, now boasting more than five hundred students.

Right
*Let us have faith that right makes might, and in that faith
let us dare to do our duty as we understand it.* Lincoln

17ᵗʰ May 2015

Pidge's head bobs up over the leafy violet patch under the jacaranda, peering, checking the territory. He's taken to hiding between the leaves – he's done his best and leaves it to other family members to sort things out. He's done with the challenges of defending the pecking order and holding on to territorial gains in the onslaught of uninvited piping shrikes. He's raised a family, it's their turn to squabble over territory and seed, but unlike his younger self, the rest of his brood aren't stayers, deserting at the first sign of trouble.

In a recent attack a dominant piping shrike stormed over to the water bowl and scared Pidge out of his wits. I don't recall a battle having been so fierce before. Pidge, startled and confused was already contending with one of his kind, intent on establishing superiority, while the dominant shrike stormed around him demanding his rights. Even the next-door cat climbed the fence to watch proceedings and teetering on top caught my eye to assure, *I'm only looking, I won't pounce!* The shrike continues to strut around the rest of the pigeon family, grown to large proportions in the bountiful spring, with a formidable air until all take flight. Except Pidge, of course.

Recovered from the last shrike versus pigeon incident, Pidge seems more cautious, or perhaps he's considering retirement, choosing to conserve his energy. His tiny head raises above the violets eyeing the scenario around the water bowl curiously. Peering with sidelong glances to make sure the flock have dispersed, a glint of sunlight in his eye, he boldly ventures out and pecks nonchalantly at stray seeds – less effort, more wisdom. Before long two piping shrikes join him but determined to remain unperturbed by their atrocious bossiness, he ignores them knowing he has as much right here as anyone else. He's earned his place, by far surpassing the bravado of his brothers and sisters. I understand.

When first married and learning to drive became a necessity I applied for my driver's licence. As a new driver I stuck to back roads on my way to the shopping centre. The hardest part was backing out of the driveway into Cross Road, one of Adelaide's main arterial roads a stone's throw from the corner of South Road, the busiest and longest road in our suburbs. Even forty years ago it was exceptionally challenging to drivers. Years on it acquired a bridge (to take the main flow of traffic over Cross Road) and a new name, *the Emerson Crossing*.

Like the Pidge, I didn't like to take chances, only shopping on certain days and times when traffic was at a low ebb. I backed out with my first car, a blue Morris Minor, then sidled into the middle lane to make a quick right-hand turn into a side street before the major intersection and toddled along beside the railway line to the local shopping centre, via the back route.

One thing standing me in good stead in those early driving days were the words of my driving instructor – a no-nonsense, generous but assertive woman who unknowingly, in my weeks of driver training, passed on advice lasting my whole life. It was *in the moment* wisdom which, apart from being useful for driving still serves me well today. I quietly assert myself in life with her helpful mantras, *you have as much right on the road as anyone else*. And, *if you're going to go, GO.* Or, *if you're going to stop,*

STOP! Also, in the early days, in response to unruly passengers in the back seat, usually misbehaving children, *pull over and STOP if safe to do so!* The latter was most useful when one day my cheeky boys were infuriatingly loud and squabbling in the back seat.

The look on their surprised faces would have melted even the hardest heart when I stopped and asked them to get out. I invited them back on board. Needless to say, there was no sound from them for the rest of the trip.

Acuteness
The keen spirit seizes the prompt occasion – makes the thought start into instant action, and at once plans and performs, resolves and executes. Hannah More

27th May 2015

The early bird gets the worm! No, not necessarily! The pigeon's relatives spend so much time sorting each other out invariably many of the seeds are missed. Fed up with their shenanigans, Pidge bides his time among the clumps of violets under the jacaranda. When the squabbling for pecking order ceases and the free-loaders leave, he returns and pecks with tranquillity – a seed here, another there; focus is key.

May foreshadows winter in a garden hushed with a mist of warmth, opening buds prematurely, long before spring begins. The red hibiscus flowering radiantly in its pot waits for a designated place in the garden. The *Diamante del Sol,* a South American migrant, usually pink and vibrant alongside boastful geraniums relishing their sunny spots, waits patiently for spring. The last days of autumn alert me to an unexpected and surprising conclusion. This period of laid-back living has manifested in me a compelling urge to refocus. *How can that be?* Well, it appears that luxuriating for too long has led to procrastination which sits uncomfortably in me and demands I return to activity.

Like Pidge, finding the cover of the foliage under the jacaranda more attractive than sorting out unruly fledglings, this patch of land has restored balance into my life. When ready he emerges contentedly to peck at remaining seed, and, taking a feather out of his plumage, I'll emerge and seek sustenance and renewed purpose in retirement.

Goodbyes

*One struggle more and I am free from pangs
that rend my heart in twain; one last long sigh to love and thee,
then back to busy life again.* Byron

17th September 2015

The continuing coolness has replaced my need to be outdoors. Though the vibrancy of spring is in the air, winter has not yet decided to let go. Viewing the expanse of garden through my bedroom window, after having darted outside to dutifully provide seed for feathered friends, I ponder at my desk.

In a life of enormous change and in equal measure periods of settling, I find myself asking, *how well have I let things go?* And, *how deep and satisfying are my goodbyes?* The answers are immediate. I haven't given my goodbyes the attention they deserve. In contrast, my hellos to new circumstances and events extract from me the full measure of my capacities – commitment, determination and endurance. I become aware of this pattern running through most of my life. I seem to harbour a subconscious need to leave an old established life as if there is nothing left to do, only old routines, habits and daily life repeating from one day to the next.

I count on my fingers and in my head. Yes, no doubt about it, every six or seven years I move on. How extraordinary! The great migratory journey from Italy to Australia in 1955 followed by constant relocation to find suitable housing in the new land, trained me well. At age twelve, after years in various rental accommodation, the family was rewarded with a home and a first mortgage – our first bricks and mortar house set on a small block of land in the eastern suburbs of Adelaide. Although more settled than I'd been in my earlier childhood and on the verge of becoming a teenager, six years on I'm on the move again to marry the would-be father of two boys. We live near the sea for almost seven years before we divorce and the house is sold.

This small home with its tiny pergola overlooking a quaint garden has come up to its six-year mark. As the spring whittles away winter to herald in newness, I sense a resurgence of old patterns – the old need to dislodge complacency and move on to my next hello! October has always been incredibly difficult at many levels. Invariably, if unplanned changes happen in my life they land on October's horizon.

I returned from my country property to South Australia via Tasmania in October 2005. My former husband accompanied me across the sea in the Spirit of Tasmania and drove me from Melbourne to Adelaide in my trusty Toyota Camry to begin life anew, and alone, in Cape Jervis – a windy place on the tip of South Australia across from Kangaroo Island. At the time I'd no idea that years on I'd be blown across the sea to live there for a while.

I don't know what this month will bring but like the Pidge, with renewed energy, I'm ready to create and draw in new abundance.

Providence
Warms in the sun, refreshes in the breeze,
glows in the stars, and blossoms in the trees. Pope

29th October 2015

The little green parrots eat the last of the loquats, once yellow and bountiful now greatly diminished – the feed of many birds. I like loquats but fiddly to eat I lazily leave the tasty pickings to them. Pigeons prefer seed and, unlike hungry natives, peck randomly. Having eaten their way to lower branches parrots often backtrack to check if they've missed any morsels, or if jostled aside by cousins invading their space.

It's joyful to watch as they systematically create an eating trail to lower branches, springing rhythmically from one branch to the next amid tweeting excitement. The uppermost fruit has almost disappeared while below it waits to be devoured. I hadn't noticed their curious eating pattern and now begin to understand the purpose of their squabbling – it's a process in the same way we organise food on our plate. Some sort out veg from other food, or squash peas into mashed potatoes before eating.

The harmonious flock nibble with chirpy little sounds of delight, tail up head down, vibrant greens and yellows only visible in movement. The art of camouflage so brilliant I'm surprised when a flurry of wings reacting to noise reveal their whereabouts, or in this case, a predator disturbing the flock. The next door cat has leapt over the fence and landed a metre or so below the branches on the roof of the small garden shed. Fascinated by the activity, he settles on his haunches watchfully and hopefully – a cat with great expectations!

Perceptions
*The more sand has escaped from the hour-glass of our life,
the clearer we should see through it.* Richter

3rd November 2015

I like butterflies and watch them gracefully flit from one fragrant sweet bloom to the next, of which there are quite a few this year. Moths, appearing heavier and slightly awkward in flight, come out at sundown and persist during the night. Not true!

The lovely white butterfly flowing in and around my lavender bush is a cabbage moth and flitters in broad daylight. I remember these delicate little creatures from childhood. Somewhere deep in memory I sit in long grass beside a bush of wispy flowers, above me a hover of white butterflies. Moths? To me they'll always be butterflies.

Life often surprises me with what I perceive to be one thing because of its name, then find it's another. A long time before I became an observer, I thought Pidge was a pigeon, which of course he is, but I'd no idea he was a particular kind – a turtle dove. Although I immediately admired his spirited personality, knowing he belonged to the more delicate group of his species made him all the more likeable. Doves possess a number of admirable qualities such as the attribute of peacefulness which I'd initially failed to see in him because I focussed on his feistiness. Within some cultures parents name their children according to a quality they wish them to attract or develop in their lives, or give them a name with an already defined quality hoping they'd grow into it.

I hope Pidge has forgiven me for typecasting him. Perhaps my humble seeds have offered compensation. Names sometimes get in the way of how we see things, or indeed, people. For instance, you may have had an amazing school teacher with a name you've never forgotten. Or on the other hand, a teacher you'd rather forget. Unfortunately, or fortunately, depending on how you look at it, our past experiences hold subconscious connotations determining how we behave in the present. I constantly test my perception of things and ask, *am I living in the present or am I living somewhere in my head?*

Retrospection
Pleasure is the flower that fades;
remembrance is the lasting perfume. Boufflers

7th November 2015

My tiny back yard has the power to draw me back to the much larger piece of land I'll always remember. A bushland property where dawns and dusks beckoned and welcomed me into the sway of wind where I allowed nature to claim my senses. Sundarra, like a much-loved teacher has taught me so much about nature, nurturing and resilience.

I watch a tiny bird evade the bird bath Pidge has reclaimed to teeter delicately on the tap to drink from the dripping hose nozzle. A far cry from the precious drops captured in a steel can from a tap in arid country where drought-challenged kangaroos took their fill from the remains of water pumped up to tanks from the Bonyaricall Creek. Where birds in a flurry of excitable wings like flowers in a florist shop would dip and sip from this strategically placed *birdbath*. Wood ducks needing more, skimmed into midsummer's ever-receding dam in the middle of parched Mallee land, sputtering and soaring in frenzied flight when the resident fox slunk stealthily closer with purposeful precision.

Often, I'd stand on the small hilly mound I named Sundarra Rise, formed from remnants of dirt dug from the ground to create the hollow for the dam. There, high above the flat land denuded by heavy-hooved strangers, I learned to love the wind caressing my face, streaming through my hair and swivelling through eucalypts, black box trees and giant river gums. The year after we bought the land (though I always felt I was only the guardian, not its owner) and the cattle had gone back to its owner, wild grasses and myriads of bush plants and tiny swamp daisies burst triumphantly from the fragile soil encouraged by an iota of rain.

In this pocket of a suburban garden, I observe and reflect like I did in Sundarra where true stillness and silence made me more aware of nature and its offerings. I've reminisced all too often about that land; but how could I not when its beauty and isolation became a powerful teacher.

I'd have happily stayed for years to witness the changes in the natural world wrought by time and the incredibly unpredictable weather conditions, becoming aware of them only when I visited years later – the familiar tracks washed away in the last flood. I wonder if, the ability to sit for long periods in a suburban garden to observe and learn from the Pidge's quirky nature would have escaped me, if not for country-living.

Principle

Let us cling to our principles as the mariner clings to his last plank when night and tempest close around him. Adam Woolever

8th November 2015

It's quite possible that the entourage of pigeons so entrenched in the daily ritual have sustained me rather than me sustaining them with the few seeds I scattered daily over the last year. I've come to know them, and they me. Was there a time when birds didn't matter as much? Yes, there was and I'm a little grieved to admit it.

I became a vegetarian years ago, not necessarily because of regard for animal life, as many yogis do. Vegetarianism wasn't an ethical decision for me. It was really about gaining strength in my body and aiding digestion. As I got deeper into yoga, meditation and vegetarianism I found myself developing a more profound view about animals and their treatment. Living in the country as a vegetarian was difficult because some of the locals were animal farmers and they thought I was strange. My husband at the time worked for a mining company and at one of their Christmas functions it became apparent as soon as we walked into the outdoor venue, what was on the menu – a scorched lamb naked and forlorn beside an enormous side of beef on a roasting spit, needing no imagination to see what kind of animal it had belonged too.

Empty plates in hand we lined up for our meal, fortunately the roasted vegetables were served first, the meat was right at the other end of the trestle table with a man carving it. Good, I thought, *I'll just fill up with vegetables*. Wrong! Given a teeny carrot, a small potato and three green string beans, I asked the young girl who was serving if I could have more since I was vegetarian and wasn't having any meat. The girl, who must have been about sixteen, looked at me her faced contorted in confusion and said, "That's all you're getting for now. If you don't have meat, that's your choice. After you've eaten you can come back and have more if there's any vegetables left." There were several times in social gatherings where I went hungry, few in the country had any idea about vegetarianism. Even the hospitality industry resisted; explaining I couldn't eat the meat but would have the vegetables I was told, *we don't serve meals that way*.

Returning from country life I readily accepted an invitation to a barbecue telling my newly acquainted friends I was vegetarian. *Oh, there'll be plenty of salads* they said. But when charred, delicate, pencil-thin bones were set on a platter before me, my heart broke and the fragments hung heavily in my chest. I'd explained that my sensitivities weren't constrained to my stomach. It was as if they hadn't understood and knew this wasn't a deliberate personal attack – after all, with the exception of the hostess they were strangers.

I watched as one by one they presided over this travesty, their light-heartedness and jollity confirming their lack of understanding *Oh, I love their crunchy bones.* I tried to release the cold shadow taken hold of me and shifted my gaze above the perfectly formed birds. I hadn't realised until the moment the platter of easily identified charred pigeons without feathers were put in front of me, how the many years of being a vegetarian had impacted on me. The creatures before me had once enjoyed full flight in a glorious sky and that's all I could think of. I calmly stood and made my apologies, *I'm sorry, I don't feel very well,* and left.

Solitude

I love to be alone. I never found the companion that was so companionable as solitude. Thoreau

9th November, 2015

Suburban land is different! Though my garden is charming and inviting it does not anchor me; the surrounding activity beyond my back yard constantly urges me to be part of it while I try to maintain my centre of peace. Intuitively, I feel that at any time I may move on and leave it behind without the connection I had for Sundarra, my country home.

Pidge has shown me the importance of claiming territory, which is exactly what I've done here, but he's also subtly reminded me about belonging. Whether squabbling or sharing with feathered siblings or friends, he belongs to his flock and they to him, and this will continue until the end of his cycle. I still sense deeply within me that this pocket of a garden is not where I belong, though I have ownership it has not claimed me in the way Sundarra had. Though mortgage papers and title deeds proved I owned it I felt rather that the land had claimed me and I was merely it's guardian.

Sundarra lives on in my mind as vivid today as it was decades ago when I left to resume my city-dweller lifestyle. I still see clearly the early morning mists and vibrant dusks of the Mallee land I once called home. It holds me in the same embrace it held me years ago as if I'd left only yesterday.

City friends couldn't understand how I lived such a solitary existence though I explained that I never felt isolated on the seven-hundred acre plus property; simply, its vast beauty and stillness wrapped around me up like a warm comforting blanket and kept me safe. I thought I'd let it go, but no, almost a decade on it draws me back. Perhaps some places sit in the heart so deeply that it's virtually impossible to remove them. I never tire of writing of its unique beauty. My Sundarra home was where, for the first time in my life, I felt I truly belonged. Strange, for a person born on a northern Italian island in the Adriatic Sea! In this diary, filled with quiet reflective moments of what is and has been, how many times have I mentioned Sundarra?

How many times have my reminiscences drawn me back to extraordinary times, to an extraordinary land, the experience unique and unrepeatable in my suburban garden? There's an urge within me to dig deeply into the past, to resurrect and feel the experience once again, to anchor its wisdom in my present and share it with others.

Country Victoria 2000-2005

Lessons from Sundarra

I thought leaving city life behind to migrate to the bush would be easy. The only easy thing about this was the decision to do it. I just wanted a simple life! On a former overgrazed sheep property, the acreage divided into land suitable for someone searching for a quiet life, namely me, I began to build strength and resilience. The flat land of over seven hundred acres was exactly what I needed to regenerate and de-stress.

On an imaginary horizon an idyllic dream hovered inviting me to spend time in nature undisturbed by the pressures of a modern world. I needed a place where I could rely on personal resources to expand my counselling, meditation and yoga practices into a career, a space of balance and harmony. The Victorian Mallee, where peace and tranquillity turned into medicine for the soul became that place.

Months into the first year of bush living I find myself in a freezing large weatherboard house that had looked so inviting in warmer weather. I sit in the nicely refurbished open-space kitchen huddled over a tiny LPG gas heater attempting to meditate. My dream of listening to bird song or the swish of wind in the eucalypts overshadowed by the thundering diesel-powered generator in the galvanised iron shed next to the house. My senses, reeling with the reverberating noise, yearn not for the tranquillity of nature but what I need most, heat. This was only the beginning of so many things I was yet to learn about country living.

Regardless of the season, early mornings even in summer would often bring cool river mists which dispersed by mid-morning along with the first layer of clothing. By lunch time another layer would join the latter, then early evening everything was reversed. Really hot days were unbearable and fortunately few and far between – air conditioning came courtesy of early evening breezes. Completely off-grid, electrical cooling had a long wait for our budget to include solar panel installation. Without the distractions of suburbia, I had plenty of time to ask myself if I'd made the right move.

I first set foot on this land when the real estate agent pulls off the main road and unlatches the large farm gate opening onto a long narrow dirt track. He'd driven slowly and deliberately up the track, wide enough for his 4WD sedan, not wanting to stir up the dusty remains of a long summer. I'd glanced from side to side taking in the flurries of black box trees and lignum bushes spread sporadically across the cracked Mallee earth. Around a bend we surprised a mob of kangaroos snoozing in late afternoon sun.

Where's the house? I wondered. 'Wow, how big is this property?' I asked thinking, *we'll never be able to afford it.* At that point a somewhat large transportable weather-board house with a return veranda needing a lick of paint, came into view. Set high above the ground on grey concrete blocks it was simple and honest and I liked it immediately. I learned later it was a flood-prone land. Delaying his response the real estate agent said laconically, 'It's been on the market about two years, maybe the couple will be willing to negotiate, they're from Adelaide too.'
'But, how big is the property?' I persisted.
'Seven hundred and fifteen acres,' he said with a practised casual air.

No way! I couldn't even *imagine* owning that much land. The me of the suburban quarter acre turned to ask, 'How much?

Walking from the car toward the back veranda he called over his shoulder, 'two hundred and sixty thousand.' It didn't seem possible that a house with acreage, cost the equivalent of a suburban property? *There must be a catch!* 'They're home,' he called again. I braced to meet the owners, obviously they did things differently in the country; suburban sellers and prospective buyers don't meet!

My idyllic first meeting of the land I name Sundarra was soon replaced with reality – living without electricity. The diesel generator housed in a shed next to the homestead, the only power source, emanated lingering chemical fumes and played havoc with my already fragile sinuses. Its persistent rattle grew to gigantic proportions reverberating from the shed and emptying into the tranquillity of the land. I was beyond grateful when it moved to a small purpose-built outbuilding further away. The noise diminished but didn't disappear so I use it sparingly.

Despite coming face to face with the sometime harsh reality of country living my initial instincts about this land never leaves me. Here my senses become alive when I see ringbarked trees, a process of land clearing for farming and grazing, feeling the grief of the land. Here I awaken to the wisdom of respecting and conserving nature in all its forms. When I return to suburban life, I leave behind a large part of my heart together with a Trust for Nature Covenant to protect the land for all time.

Creation
Silently as a dream the fabric rose;
No sound of hammer or of saw was there.   Cowper

2000

Answers to *What am I doing here?* land with soft footfalls in a corner of my heart whenever I sit among giant river gums, some barely alive. Long roots half embedded in loamy clay dirt on the banks of the Bonyaricall Creek speak of better times, days when the Murray River flooded with abundant rain and new growth peeked from nooks and crannies of fledgling roots. The ancient trees, remnants of their former selves, tell tales of previous lives, of people camped along the mighty river nourished by all nature offers.

Settled beneath a favourite river gum from which a canoe has been carved by the original Aboriginal inhabitants, the wind becomes my friend as it whistles through canopies of eucalypts reaching with spindly arms to the sky. I feel at peace. It's as if the river giants' gnarled roots diverting into the creek seeking water for continued survival, welcome me, another survivor on this precious land. I'm in the same place where ancients once skilfully carved the bark of eucalypts for canoes, coolamons and other necessities and lived respectfully alongside nature.

I'm slowly discovering that bush living requires a certain character, an undefined personality recognisable only when it appears. As a city dweller, it took me several months, maybe longer, to notice the differences in myself and my outlook on life prompted by the natural environment. Deluded by the trappings of urban living, the call of the country seemed the perfect solution for slowing to an easy, simple pace. At first, I didn't envisage anything deeper.

Gum trees sidling along creek beds and the banks of the lazy Murray River bordering our flat land of native grasses and lignum bushes between smatterings of black box trees, offered me alternatives to suburbia only because I was prepared to take a leap of faith. I could have so easily missed this opportunity. Fleeting moments in rural bushland, visiting or holidaying wouldn't have been enough to tug the heartstrings to a contemplative way of life. With no conveniences at my doorstep, or stimulations abducting my brain and propelling it along with my body over the stress threshold, it drew me to alternatives I may never have considered.

Character

Fine natures are like fine poems; a glance at the first two lines suffices for a guess into the beauty that waits you if you read on. Bulwer-Lytton

2000

What was it exactly that gave me enough strength to uproot myself and spurn me on this kind of living, in isolated conditions away from family, friends, a successfully growing stress management practice and all I'd know in my life? The answer isn't a simple one, yet, in a way it is – meditation. If I hadn't taken the time to cultivate stillness, with what I once considered a strange obscure practice, I would not have envisioned new horizons and the courage to move towards them. And, as always, it's not just one thing facilitating change, it is a number of precipitating events rolling into one another.

So, as I immerse myself in the endless tasks of preparation to turn the homestead into a smallish retreat centre I receive a phone call, a voice taking me back to the first time I heard it on a telephone message machine. It was the doctor who introduced me to meditation. She was travelling into Victoria on her way to Sydney, and wondered if I was ready to accept visitors – herself and her partner for an overnight stay. *Yes*, I say then, when I get off the phone with the noise of the generator thundering in the background, I panic and contemplate calling her back to say, *No*.

As I prepare the two single beds in the rudimentary spare room, I think of how this remarkable woman came into my life when I was at my lowest ebb. Someone who'd met fleetingly at a party had given me her phone number. *Ring her* she urged. I had nothing to lose. My health was on a rapid downward slide. The job which had sustained my talents and finances, non-existent. Every day was a struggle with periods of chronic fatigue leaving me to wonder what was happening in my life. Here I was in the smart art deco home I acquired with the settlement of my second divorce. The Midas touch gone, the will to create gone, replaced by an insidious downward spiral drawing me further through a trapdoor where it was cold and dark. But it was here, in this small dismal place, that I begin my search for meaning.

I turn a page of a tired, wet local *rag* (newspaper) I'd rescued from my front lawn and read *"When you get to your lowest and you can't go any lower, a trapdoor opens up and you fall into the light."* I find the phone number scribbled down at the party and dial with trembling fingers. A recorded articulate smoothly gentle voice responds saying she is unavailable. My mood sinks even lower. *Ha! Another doctor, busy, stressed like the rest of us.* Being frugal, I never waste a call, I leave a message not for a moment believing the voice on the other end would emerge as a real person, and go for a walk.

On return I glance at my phone next to the front door. There is a light, a tiny blinking light signalling a message on my machine. I listen to the same clear soothing voice: *I'm sorry Anita that I wasn't home to answer your call when you rang, please do call again.* Then there is a pause, *I hope you are alright!*

I can't help thinking: *A real person, a doctor who doesn't mind giving out her home phone number, a person who cares enough to respond, to a perfect stranger.* Her few words touch me deeply in that place where no-one has been for a very long time. I sit on the floor cradling the phone and cry.

I step back and admire the finishing touches to the spare room my friend will occupy overnight. With the generator turned off for her imminent arrival I hear once again the melodic calls of the butcher birds calling to each other and hope nature and a wholesome evening meal will make up for lack of facilities in Sundarra. The landline rings again, the voice is unmistakenly hers; they've made it to the next town, found a motel for an overnight stay, too tired to detour and travel our way.

Wisdom
Wisdom and eloquence are not often united. Victor Hugo

2000

I see a little nursing home on the edge of town and thinking it might be an inroad to meeting people, I go along to volunteer my talents. I soon discover that the *senior* residents, the ones living here the longest, don't like their residence being referred to as a *nursing home*. It's an *aged care hostel, do you mind!*

I also realise that my counselling and teaching professions don't give me status or exclusive rights to anything in this place (even though I don't expect them to). What I do find is the fact they work against me. In my first *Writing about Life Experiences* session, I scan the room full of grey and white-haired budding writers. The motley group aged from sixty and beyond smile in unison. What am I going to teach these people who have life experiences way beyond mine? Well, at least they look friendly!

I begin with, 'Well now, we'll start with a list, just like a shopping list. Number the items from one to whatever and list the most significant events of your life.' A few papers shuffle, pens tap, notebooks flip open, faces look at me expectantly. There is a long silence until a rather perplexed woman with thick glasses on the end of her nose stares at me quizzically and asks, 'Can you give us an example of significant events?'

'Yes, yes of course. What about the day you married, or the day you first saw your grandchild.'

'Ok, I get it,' the woman responds, then quickly adds, 'what about the day you flew your own aircraft, trekked the Himalayas or slaughtered your first pig or…'

'Oh, yes, yes, of course, anything like that would be interesting,' I say feeling myself turn a bright shade of red.

The *senior residents*, as they liked to be called, didn't quite take to the information I offered, at their age they knew everything they needed to know. At the end of another session introducing the group to poetry writing, feeling quite satisfied that the group enjoyed it, I ask,
'Shall we do this again next week?'

'Well, dear lady,' one of the *senior* seniors said, 'When old meets new, you must remember that we came to this session for you, not the other way around!'

Perseverance

*There is no royal road to anything. One thing at a time,
all things in succession. That which grows fast withers as rapidly;
that which grows slowly endures.* J.G. Holland

2000

The *senior* seniors in the local retirement home obviously didn't need my writing workshops. Surprisingly, for a small community, Robinvale appeared to be an enormous melting pot of people from a vast array of cultures from around the world. Aboriginal people mixed mainly with their own as did people from other cultures, finding comfort with those they were familiar with. There seemed to be a certain reserve about connecting with each other or with visitors or itinerant workers on property who were here one day and gone the next. The local hotel I'd heard, was the only place with some degree of *mixing* and then, after *a few drinks*, anything was likely to happen.

The Italians and Greeks, having lived here almost as long as the *Aussies* who'd been offered soldier settlements land after World Wars, seeming to comfortably rub shoulders with everyone, appeared to have large land holdings and more monetary sway than many. I wondered if the Vietnamese, Polynesians and Asians who dutifully worked and lived thriftily would one day step up. The signs were already there in the main street in the form of local businesses who everyone availed themselves of: a very popular Vietnamese restaurant, an Asian grocery store selling everything from Chinese cabbages to slip-on sandals and glitzy trinkets, a store and meeting hall frequented by the Tongan community with amazingly beautiful singing voices.

Despite losing a degree of confidence with efforts to attract people to yoga classes the *Taurus* in me did not give up. Swan Hill with a larger population was my next go-to – one hundred and twenty-five kilometres, an hour and a quarter drive away, was a marathon; I'd never driven so far in one stint. I decided for my first journey to another country town I needed a companion and invited the fourteen-year-old from a neighbouring family to accompany me with a promise of lunch and *nosey* into the dress shops.

Apparently, there *was* a resident yoga teacher in Swan Hill but her frequent trips to India left classes without yoga. No problem, I'd call her. Surely a town with a population of over 12,000 could accommodate two yoga teachers. My yoga style, different from hers, could provide a choice. Yoga, after all, isn't just about teaching postures and sequences it's about imparting wise, peaceful life-learning philosophies to students. My first telephone call to her upset and confused me. She related that she'd spent *many years building up classes* and emphasised how difficult it had been to attract *country people* to yoga. The conversation left me feeling depressed; the outcome wasn't in keeping with yogic philosophy.

From my spacious study cum-therapy room I scan with weepy eyes the immeasurable beauty of the flat Mallee landscape through the spacious window. Somewhat arid in places and infinitely abundant in others with flurries of black box trees and bushes, it draws me to the foreground where the rustic garden boasts snatches of lawn, watered sparingly over the summer months to keep the dust down. Centrally placed are two small rectangular plots of hardy native plants and lavender bushes bordered by pine logs, an enigma in this part of the country.

A resident magpie happily pecking away and scratching for grubs stops suddenly when a swooping black shadow lands beside her and starts to nonchalantly mirror her movements. The magpie, full-breasted at the intrusion, baulks at sharing her space with this dark stranger and advances on the sizeable crow. He stands still, solidly maintaining his presence for a moment, then, ignoring her, continues to peck at tiny offerings in the ground. Again, the magpie advances, again he ignores her. Obviously, his intention isn't to antagonise but to make the most of the slim pickings brought up by the previous evening's watering. His boldness is clearly giving me a message – *don't give up, remember the Earth belongs to everyone*. How simple, there's my answer!

Swan Hill became my greatest pleasure and delight where I established three classes, hired a room for counselling from a natural therapy centre and made long-term friendships. Years later settled back in Adelaide, I revisited and one of my former students organised a reunion lunch at the paddle steamer restaurant on the Murray River. It was wonderful to know that six years on they still remembered and appreciated the yoga classes and our time together.

Nature
Nature, like a kind and smiling mother,
lends herself to our dreams and cherishes our fancies. Victor Hugo

2001

The Mallee, usually dry in early Autumn with a beauty all of its own, at any moment can become victim to the weather's whims and subject to immediate change and transformation. After two days and nights of rain the land became a magically green carpet abundant with wildlife and birds I'd never seen before: yellow regent parrots who usually shoot over the land in jet-like formations stop, forage and roost, emus bring families and kangaroos increase in numbers. The red topsoil of the higher land around the homestead drains quickly but lower ground holds water for a couple of weeks encouraging the visiting creatures to stay around a few days longer. What an amazing experience to be caught in the middle of a spectacular storm surrounded by so much land. Feeling both exposed and mesmerised I walk from window to window peering at the results of gale force winds howling through lignum bushes, black box and eucalypts dotted across the land and around and under our timber-framed home, wailing eerily like lost souls set free.

It's almost funny to think that in my solid brick home in Adelaide, surrounded by people, amenities and at-call services, protected from the elements and possible adversity, I didn't feel as safe. In this bushland environment, one moment surrounded by magical beauty and in the next in the middle of unbridled nature I feel vulnerable, but secure. When infrequent storms raged around my suburban house, the outdoors less visible from small and larger curtained windows, I found myself fearing the worst. Would the roof fly off, the house and garden suffer damage from falling branches, electricity wires and windswept debris? I felt vulnerable being unable to fully observe what was happening, not knowing what precautions to take and what needed attention.

In Sundarra, the astonishing opportunity to follow the storm through large curtainless windows allows me to interpret its messages, gauge its severity and determine the level of safety. In the homestead, on concrete block high above the flood plain, I feel there's no real threat of flooding, while the sound of the galvanised roof withstanding the heavy rain and bombardment of wind tells me, if the roof hasn't blown off already it's not likely to. Positioned in the middle of the property the homestead, with so much space around it is free from flying debris, so different from a suburban house in a compacted garden, a tiled roof camouflaging sound and prone to lifting in severe winds. Here, in a house above the ground the wind flows freely around and underneath, unlikely to do much damage. It's true, fears are more damaging than reality.

Regardless of nature's wild adventures, including some close encounters with snakes who have a preference to avoiding humans, Sundarra instils in me an incredible sense of having arrived in my true home. I'm learning that re-connecting with the natural environment is vital to my human functioning and that mother earth needs me as much as I need her. I'm truly aware, for the first time ever in a face-to-face situation, how this land's resources have been drained and of my responsibility to help regenerate it.

In the scheme of things, in rural Victoria this is just a small plot of land; how has nature been compromised in many such parcels of land? According to the agent for Trust for Nature, who visited our property recently and did a comprehensive survey of plant and animal life, twothirds of Victoria's natural vegetation has been removed. There's no doubt about it, *Mother Nature* is in crisis, balance has been well and truly tipped and her need is greater than ours.

At dawn, the paddock beyond the glass sliding door at the back of the homestead transforms with light, rising from a sun-kissed misty horizon slowly unfurling hues of colour into the eastern sky. While at dusk the western sky treats us to the splendored orange-gold only a sunset can create. The time in-between draws my attention to the demanding work the natural land needs for regeneration, and the numerous chores and maintenance tasks the property needs. Acclimatising to diesel generator power, lack of rainfall for water tanks and the limited amenities available to us would have taken my all had I not been caught between magnificence and hard work.

Summer has been long, hot, dry and demanding on the physical energy needed to turn Sundarra with limited infrastructure, electricity and water supply into a wellness retreat centre. But no matter how tough life gets I can't lose sight of the dream, my motivating force.

Over the last few weeks private clients have trickled in for the programs I offer. And I'm encouraged by locals ambling into yoga classes and if not by their interest, promising to *give it a go* soon – everything takes time! *It's a two-way street*, I tell myself. They're taking time to get to know me and I'm gradually getting used to them and their country ways.

I've stopped making comparisons between my old life with all its services and commodities and my bush lifestyle knowing it's something that cannot be fashioned, only experienced. I'm feeling hopeful now Sundarra offers basic accommodation with bunk beds, nutritious food, daily yoga and meditation and endless walks in acres of a tranquil bush setting in a river environment, former Adelaide clients will join me for retreats.

Gifts

If we will take the good we find, asking not questions, we shall have heaping measures. The great gifts are not got by analysis. Everything good is on the highway. Emerson

2002

I'd never owned a dog so when *Blue-Dog* came to live with us I was excited, and just a little anxious. I'd met him before and immediately formed a strong opinion of him; handsome and intelligent, with a gentle, happy nature he immediately responded to kindness. He'd been employed by the Robinvale Golf Course to guard the shed and its contents of tractors, mowers and other valuable equipment. Before we bought Sundarra I got to know him on my daily walks around the golf course. I didn't think he'd ever seen a woman up close, especially one with a long skirt, and at first was timid but soon graciously accepted me and learnt to put up his paw in greeting when I visited.

My husband, introduced to him when he became Greens Manager was told, *stay clear of him, he's vicious,* as he lunged at him from the end of a heavy metal chain. They hadn't given him a name, only a job, so he called him *Blue-Dog* and they became inseparable. He'd spent most of his life at the end of a chain but this hadn't changed his nature. When my husband left for a new job with a local mining company he asked one thing of his former employer. And so Blue-Dog came to stay!

The day he came to live with us at Sundarra was probably the first time he'd ever been taken on a leisurely drive and seen paddocks with cattle, sheep and horses and, the first time he'd ever had a home. As he bounded off my husband's Ute he looked joyful, with a face and wagging tail saying it all, and though I'd doubted that dogs could smile, I had to admit he was smiling!

Over the next few weeks, he needed to learn how to walk sensibly beside us. Often, he strained at the leash to pursue what was at the end of many enticing scent trails to chase the abundant wildlife from the tiniest grasshopper to mobs of kangaroos. Most of the time we weren't quite sure who was taking who for a walk. But at all times he was polite and obedient, just extremely overjoyed at all these wondrous sensations in his new life. Eventually he slowed down enough for me to take hold of the leash without being carried away understanding there was discipline in freedom.

On a hot summer's day I heard him barking excitedly from our farm shed – Blue-Dog's temporary home until he got used to sleeping inside our laundry. I didn't want him so far away from the house, though, with the dog run strewn across the yard he could go in and out as he pleased. His long chain, a temporary restraint, was attached by a rope to the run during the day so he didn't feel confined to the shed. I'd often have a cup of tea outdoors with Blue-Dog, talk to him, tickle his tummy and pat him while he sat respectfully beside me. How he got the reputation of being a *fierce* dog I'll never know – all he needed was a little love!

Investigating the barking I find he's cornered a *stumpy tail* lizard looking quite cross and a trifle dusty on the shed's dirt floor. I order him to get back and I'm amazed that he obeys immediately as the poor creature waddles away. A few days after this *stumpy tail* incident, I race out of the shower with a sense of urgency, thinking I'd heard him bark. It's quiet, too quiet, and deep in my gut I get the feeling Blue-Dog is in trouble. Out in the yard I can see he's at the end of his chain in a far corner of the shed. I move closer and freeze when I spot a large angry brown snake at his feet.

I keep my distance and call to him frenetically. He looks up for a moment but stands his ground; he's stalking, not over-excited, merely prancing around having a lovely game with this strange creature. It would be madness to try and reach him without endangering my safety so I keep my distance, yelling at him to come. Reluctantly, he does, but not before he picks up the snake in his mouth. Suddenly all fear leaves me, adrenalin thundering in my ears as I take hold of the end of his chain and yank it, screaming at him until he lets go. As I draw him closer I notice the wet patch on his head, he's been bitten.

I click his chain onto the *run* and circle the rope around a tree away from the shed to prevent him from returning to catch the fleeing snake. Thursday, good news, the vet is in town. Too heavy to lift I race into the homestead to telephone my husband working fifteen minutes' drive away. We bundle Blue-Dog into his Ute and he sits between us on the front seat, paws on my knees and tail thumping ecstatically knowing he's going for a ride.

It was so inspiring to watch both the young vet and nurse calmly and capably spring into action and clear the waiting room of clients by simply saying that Blue-Dog had been bitten by a *brown*. As people gathered their pets and left, I feel their silent wave of compassion and understanding. Between licks of approval, tail wagging constantly and amber eyes radiating with happiness, Blue-Dog is smiling. We stroke him in an effort to calm his excitement as the vet holds him gently on the table. He loves the attention, just another wonderful event in his new life, but I wish he'd stop wagging his tail pushing the poison through the rest of his body!

We quickly learn the clinic has run out of anti-venom and the closest supply is in Mildura, over an hour away. In another generous example of country spirit, a woman who'd been in the waiting room takes it upon herself to make phone calls to local property owners who keep anti-venom on their properties for their horses. But it's too late – an hour and a half later, in our arms and in the attentive tender care of the two beautiful young women, he dies, gently and without pain. Up to the very last moment of his life Blue-Dog was happy, his death sudden. In the moment of passing he looks at each of us in puzzlement asking, *what's happening to me?* Overwhelmed by a depth of feeling I can only describe as a surge of energy, we all burst into tears and embrace. The vet and nurse, who must witness so many animals in pain, were as touched as we were.

We bury Blue-Dog under a gum tree beside the dam. After heartfelt goodbyes we walk wearily back to the Ute and there, where Blue-Dog's body had lain, was a large dead butterfly with the same colour markings, an omen of transformation.

Loyalty
*Master go on, and I will follow thee, to the last gasp,
with truth and loyalty.* Shakespeare

2003

I usually turn off the generator after dark. We now have enough solar panels to sustain basic needs but must be economical with energy use in sunless days. Before bed the fridge goes off and anything plugged into power sockets pulled out. Abby, our Staffordshire terrier, sits on the back veranda steps waiting for me to head off to the generator shed, some distance away, and back again. It's a noisy old thing.

Since Arnie's arrived, he'll walk with me without any coaxing. Torch in hand and his nose on my heel I feel protected when my husband does night shift at the local titanium mines. I know this pup won't be tearing off to follow some unknown creature into the night I found Arnie on one of my visits to parents in Adelaide, a funny, warm loveable blue heeler Australian shepherd cross. The major shopping centre, five minutes' drive away, strangely enough is a respite from the traffic-congested noisy main road and the rattling bungalow with the rusty roof which is their home.

When I spotted him in the pet shop window, sitting alert, ears cocked listening to sounds around him, I couldn't go past without taking a closer look. The shop assistant wasted no time in pointing out his attributes and following quickly with *Do you want to hold him?* I knew the trick and said *no.* In a flash he was out of the cage and in her arms encouraging me to hold him. I refused again but stroked him as he snuggled into her. I walked out of the shop and saying *if he's still here after I've done all my shopping maybe then I'll hold him.* Our incredibly spoilt *Staffy* needed a companion, this could be the one.

Days later I found myself driving back to Sundarra with a small bundle of fur lazily snoozing on the back seat. At eight weeks old and unused to car travel he got quite queasy so I slotted in a few extra stops on the way home. He'd become a necessary distraction in the preceding days for both my parents; instrumental in rousing Papacci out of his self-absorbed state and giving Mammina, enthralled with the antics of this small energetic pup, opportunity to be child-like again. A week later and a six hour or more journey, with comfort breaks thrown in for both myself and little Arnie (named after the Arndale Shopping Centre), was enough for us to bond. By the time we arrived home we were inseparable, his choice not mine. The Staffordshire terrier hadn't ever been *mine,* gifted to my husband by his daughters. Staffy's have a loveable nature but unless well trained sometimes don't tolerate other dogs in their territory, even if the territory is over 700 acres, which was the case for Abby.

Arnie is different, intelligent, funny and malleable as well as loyal and protective. He has his wet nose on my heels as I walk the several metres to the generator shed to turn it on to supplement the solar power, and then back again to switch it off at bedtime. Guided by feeble torch light in the pitch black of the Australian bush back and forth to the homestead I'm under his watchful eye and wet nose. At only a few months old he's developed remarkable qualities. I'm astounded by his attention to sound, so acute he alerts me long before I hear anything and gives a warning bark. He's incredibly aware, focussed and responsive – the true mark of the Australian cattle dog. With him beside me I feel more secure than ever. He's absorbed all my training quickly and effortlessly, learnt all the tricks Abby taught him, much to her annoyance, and become a powerful presence in my life and hers. In many ways Arnie reminds me of Blue-Dog, the heeler we'd lost to snake bite.

A sizeable outside dog pen has been built, mostly for Arnie. He's our *outside* dog with exclusive rights to it except for the times Abby, the loveable pest that she is, shares it during yoga classes; a safety precaution for students who've already suffered multiple slobbering licks. Confined to the pen, the dogs bark incessantly when they arrive for yoga classes wanting to be part of the action, the whole scenario repeating when class is finished. I learnt very quickly that letting them out of the pen before they get back in their vehicles is a mistake. The chase would be on to follow cars down the track to the main gate at the highway. Abby, with short stubby legs tires easily. While Arnie, excited in pursuit, chooses not to hear my call and follows them all the way down the track to the highway. Satisfied with his little bit of fun he returns with a guilty expression, tongue lolling out, tail contritely between his legs ready to accept reprimand.

The dog pen, enough space to cavort and run in with a small shelter shed at one end, is a godsend! In there they are safe, but not from everything. One day, after students had driven off, I'm on the top step outside the back door of the homestead, about to wander over and let the dogs out when a flicker of movement in the shadow of the shed stops me. Arnie, along with Abby, barking excitedly at the gate waiting for me to open it, notices it too. I call his name to keep his attention on the gate and run quickly to unlatch it. At the edge of the shed, a snake, obviously overwhelmed with all the excitement, is frantically searching for escape.

It's a hot humid day, and there's no way I want to repeat the Blue-Dog experience, so I keep the dogs indoors for several hours. Arnie, who's rarely inside these days, enjoys the privilege immensely and makes the most of the large settee which dwarfed him as a pup. His long paws hang over one arm rest and his tail thrashes happily at the other end. One look at Abby tells me she is miffed; after all, he's in her territory, not realising this is the beginning of her quest for leadership. Arnie couldn't learn anything more from Abby, having mastered everything, even the way female dogs squat to relieve themselves, his sharp inquisitive mind is yearning for more.

Shortly after Christmas, following an aggressive assault for leadership which Arnie playfully hadn't taken seriously, a decision has to be made. The Swan Hill Council finds Arnie a new home. I pull into the vet's carpark in Swan Hill as arranged and fumble nervously with Arnie's lead securely tied to the door armrest of the back seat. The dog rescuer comes to my aid, 'Would he be okay if *I* did it?' Arnie responds with a lick. My heart breaks as he jumps up obediently into his Ute and sits obligingly looking first at me then at him with questioning soulful eyes.

Three months later I give in to the nagging thought to call the Swan Hill Council. The dog rescuer says, 'Ah yes, I remember him, a nice dog, found a good home for him, a farm in Sea Lake.' The small locality about an hour away near the Mallee Highway is well sign-posted so when I drive past to visit family in Adelaide, I'm often tempted to take a detour in the hope of seeing him again.

Beginnings
Begin whatever you have to do;
the beginning of a work stands for the whole. Ausonious

2004

Touched by sunlight streaming through the black box tree at the back door of the homestead I feel whole, the first warm spring day though its well into November. The tumultuous unpredictable weather patterns pervading September has confused nature, the people and crops of this small country town.

Eventually storms settle but the inside of me is still churning now that my husband has left, for yet another job, in another town, where he'll work and live returning on weekends. There's no point agonising over it, he's gone and nothing is ever going to be the same again. My first regular trip into town without him for a cup of coffee in the only café in town brings unnecessary attention and stares. Resolving to remain stoic in his absence I smile vaguely answering questions, *he's in a new job, not far, comes home on weekends.* Heads nod, understanding. The local titanium mine, where he'd worked after the golf course job, had closed down. He was lucky to have a job, many have been left with no future prospects.

I was happy when he excitedly told me about it, until it dawned that he'd have to live away from home. His new workplace, a local council of another country town three hour's drive away, compelled him to live weekdays in a farm hand's hut near his job. His long-awaited return on a Friday evening, dead-tired, is not conducive to conversation –he eats his evening meal without a word. Attentive and eager to reignite an emotional spark I match his silence and sit at the table waiting and watching for cues inviting me in so I can draw his heart back into mine.

The first evening back he surveys our living area, now a pristine environment in readiness for retreat visitors – everything in its right place to facilitate the movements of a small group. I feel pleased with my efforts and hope he does too since I was trying to add to our income stream. Even the dusty alcove off the kitchen area where he kept a collection of all things ancient or *deceased* looked remarkably clean. I had respected his space and not touched anything without permission, gleaned over a phone conversation when I prepared for the retreat. But he lashes out vehemently at the changes, saying it is no longer a home. Unprepared for his anger I cower and withdraw into the yoga room as if struck by a blow and try, unsuccessfully, to hold back a deluge of tears.

The question of moving hasn't come up. It makes sense, we've worked hard to maintain Sundarra; a non-working farm wouldn't sell easily during drought, or even in better times. Besides, I've yet to fulfil my dream of running it as fully established retreat centre. Anyway, it's even more difficult to sell now we'd put a covenant on it with Trust for Nature to conserve 500 acres of bushland. The paddocks around the homestead on higher ground are enough for a small agricultural business, though unfortunately, our budget wasn't enough to improve and connect a reliable irrigation system.

Courage
Courage consists not in blindly overlooking danger, but in seeing it and conquering it. Richter

2004

One of the problems I face occasionally on our huge acreage are trespassers hunting wild pigs, kangaroos or rabbits. Today, on one of my regular walks down the track to the creek, I hear the unmistakeable rumbling sound of a vehicle thundering through the bushy environment on my right. A large Ute and its occupants, obviously spotting me and with nowhere to go, pulls up in front of me.

Two young men, looking sheepish and slightly embarrassed hop out. 'Sorry, is this private property,' one asks?
'Didn't you see the fences and the signs?' I snap back.
'Ah, yeah, they were down…we're a bit lost,' he says grinning guiltily.

Not wanting to continue the conversation which was obviously going nowhere, I direct them down the track and around the creek with a warning that I'd report them if they trespassed again. As they do a three-point turn on the small track I pull my notebook out of my pocket, stand in the middle of the track, clearly visible through their rear vision mirrors, and write down their registration number. Not long after this incident I encounter more trespassers, on foot this time. I spot them through the trees where I'd put up very visible signs: Private Property – Trespassers Prosecuted. Two tall young men wearing protective canvas-type clothing, heavy boots and carrying guns with huge dogs alongside, Irish Wolf Hounds I think, also in protective garb – there's doubt in my mind what they're hunting. I confront them and they respond with silly grins feigning disbelief that, *somehow,* they find themselves on private property. After putting up a brave front to disguise my trembling heart and knees, and inwardly grumbling that my husband is absent when he's most needed, they leave retracing their footsteps.

The locals had warned me of wild pigs coming seasonally across properties to eat crops ready for picking on surrounding farms. I hadn't been fearful of these animals, only the humans firing guns aimlessly, but I'd become wary during my walks, even formulating an escape plan – if I came upon a pig I'd climb the closest tree. But I had the feeling that these animals were as keen not to be discovered as I was. I begin to understand why they are hunted, apart from preventing damage to crops, some farmers, mainly Italians, are partial to feasting on pigs and making sausages out of them.

Learning that good money is paid for feral pigs we acquire a large cage from the Department of Resources and Environment and position it on a bushy bit of land near the creek. We check the cage regularly but nothing is forthcoming, even though the titbits of food disappear, the cage remains empty – pigs are too smart to be caught. So, I continue to keep my eyes peeled for feral invaders. The only one I spot is a fox, large golden bushy tail, flamboyantly beautiful as he drinks from the dam in full view of *Sundarra Rise,* the solidified mound of loamy clay on which I do my daily yoga practice.

My son in Adelaide learns of our hunting endeavours and sends two of his mates, confirmed pig hunters he tells me, to set up camp on the property. The long weekend when they arrive blows a gale threatening to send much needed rain to the land but only succeeding in blowing down their tent repeatedly – they take shelter in our large farm shed and return to Adelaide, *pigless*. Months on, we catch sight of our first pig, literally on our doorstep. By the time we scramble out in our pyjamas he's gone. The next morning, we see him again, this time nibbling on the cabbage we've put out overnight. He's small and pink, a piglet, unlikely to do anyone any damage but by the time we open the screen door he's off across the paddock with no hope of being caught.

It's the Easter weekend, and my husband whose home from work, decides to bring the cage, placed in the middle of the property, to the back of the homestead along with loads of food scraps to entice the visiting piglet back. On Sunday morning we are rewarded. A forlorn-looking pink animal with bloodied front legs and a squinty eye, peers at us from the cage – there's no way this is a feral pig! We make enquiries in the district but no one claims ownership. He's obviously fallen off the back of a truck with a jolt, that would explain his injured front legs – livestock carriers on the Murray Valley Highway approaching the bend in front of the main gate to our property slow down hurriedly.

We keep him and call him Boris. Abbey our *staffy* befriends him and plays chasey with him, running round and round the outside of the pen we dutifully build when he outgrows the cage. One day he grabs the little tartan coat we've given her for the colder Mallee weather and Abby is no longer keen to play with him. Boris amuses himself by upending the tall water container we fill up at least twice a day to create mud baths in which he wallows contentedly. He gets larger and larger and healthier, feasting on abundant left-overs from our mainly vegetarian diet – his legs have healed and so has his eye. Boris is intelligent and funny, responding quickly to our attention but comes the day, a year or so later, he needs a new home, and so do we.

We hear of a local pig farmer who's looking for a sire and introduce him. Confirming he's a fine specimen for fathering offspring he arrives in a Ute to collect him. I watch as he places a ramp from the pen to the back of his Ute and entices Boris to walk up it by placing tasty morsels along it. He takes the first step, has a nibble, then looks up at me – he's surprisingly calm and collected as if he knows what's about to happen. I encourage him gently, and, fortunately, the pig farmer does too. As he trustingly trots onto the tray of the Ute I turn away, feeling as wounded as he is. I look on from a distance and as he's driven away, Boris turns his head toward me and eyeballs me, I cry.

When I think back on those days, I'm amazed at the courage and adventures that would never have happened if I remained in Adelaide. I'd have happily stayed on that beautiful piece of earth regardless of drought, floods, bushfire threats and other challenges, but there were reasons, despite the survival skills I was developing, I could not have stayed on the property alone. The physical energy needed to maintain the phenomenal piece of land was greatly diminished, the mortgage massive, the upkeep huge and my income minimal. Fibromyalgia and fatigue returned with a vengeance whenever my muscles engaged in physical activity.

My husband, having secured employment elsewhere yet again, his fourth job in six years, leaves me with little choice but to follow him to Tasmania to search for, I know not what. Though I'd become used to his weekly absence in his former job, the logistics of maintaining Sundarra and my new lifestyle completely without support, is out of the question. I am resourceful with smaller tasks and handle them well, like changing the enormous gas cylinder when it runs out. At dusk, in cooler months, I tread carefully the well-worn animal tracks searching for twigs and small pieces of wood for the combustion heater in the yoga/lounge room – much needed in early evening. The LPG gas heater in the kitchen and living area is small, reasonably effective but expensive to run; anyhow gas is best kept for fuelling the cooker and hot water service.

Solar panels and the diesel-charged generator do the rest, but diesel fuel too has almost doubled in price. I wonder what my city friends would think to see me walk the kangaroo trails in the cool of dusk with a green shopping bag in each hand, stopping here and there to gather kindling, careful not to create homelessness for creatures, especially slithery ones. I laugh at the thought, with grungy clothes and well-worn ankle boots, I look like a *bag lady*. With the many *brown snakes* in the area, I steer clear of bushy segments and feel reasonably safe. At times, pockets of the land compel me to stand still and listen, the energy so tangible I can touch it. I lose myself in timeless moments and with no will of their own my eyes gaze softy through mists of time to a life of long ago, so long before mine. It's this feeling of indescribable serenity which urges me to share this healing land with others.

Small groups from my former Adelaide client base visit and experience at different levels what I've attempted to describe in newsletters. Responses from visitors confirm the land of Sundarra is precious. I realise how powerfully nature has surpassed expectations, theirs and mine – the ancients and natures healing magic have touched them deeply.

Dreaming
*Dreams are the bright creatures of poems and legend,
who sport on the earth in the night season, and melt away
with the first beam of the sun, which lights grim care and stern
reality on their daily pilgrimage through the world.* Dickens

2004

When I found this idyllic place on the Murray Valley Highway seventeen kilometres from Robinvale, three months after arriving in Robinvale, it lay like an unclaimed jewel waiting for someone to pocket it. Keeping the overgrazed property safe, free from wild pigs and their trespassing hunters and restoring the gem to its former beauty wasn't in the dream beckoning on my imaginary horizon. But this diamond of Mallee earth continues to sparkle as I muster all the courage I have left.

My idealistic decision to uproot from a comfortable, almost mortgage-free home in Adelaide, to set up a retreat centre in a rural wonderland devoid of modern pressures has taken a lot out of me. Nothing could have prepared me for what has happened. Overplanning is always my downfall but in this instance, I saw only the dream and I relied on my penchant for resourcefulness and organisational skills without even thinking about it. On reflection, I may never have lived my dream if I'd put too much thought towards it.

Reality emerges slowly as I traipse through the maze of country-living challenges unlike any I've experienced as a *namby-pamby* city dweller. So many things I'd once taken for granted have reared heads and demanded attention. Traversing the terrain from the homestead via a narrow track leading to the main highway is an incredibly difficult manoeuvre in wet weather; and wet weather does indeed come after a few short months of moving in. The rain, on the undulating surface on this slip of a road leading to the Murray Valley highway having lost soil in dry summers, fills pot holes quickly. Volumes of water flood the track and roll off the edges to grey river flats on either side, not much use for farming, sustaining only sparse grasses, bushes and the odd tree. Its only when flooding abates that its beauty returns with new growth and carpets of tiny swamp daisies defying the drought. Wizened bushes, some thought extinct, rise from loamy compacted soil and scraggle the flat acreage in front of the property, the view of my wide study window; isolation bliss filled with spacious serenity.

X-ray vision can't deflect the immense satisfaction and joy I feel on remembering that fateful day, when spellbound I travelled to the homestead with the real estate agent the dusty track, which was to give me many headaches. The property, Yallumarina, initially misnamed by the previous owners after yellow box trees of which there are none, only black box trees and eucalypts, became Sundarra. Sundarra continues to give everything and more – unexpected challenges and insights into the spirit of the land and mine.

Zest for living a healthy organic life has led me to the *beautiful one* with one certainty, nature is a healer and with time this fragile land will restore, revive and regenerate.

Listening
*Nature has given to men one tongue, but two ears,
that we may hear from others twice as much as we speak.* Epictetus

2005

The day the Aboriginal elder came to visit Sundarra on my invitation she was quietly pensive. She sipped her tea and avoided eye contact unlike the first time we'd met when she opened up to share her story. We'd met in the township, in a shop where I'd been delivering candles for world peace after the *Twin Towers* bombing in America.

I felt compelled to counteract the gloom embracing this tiny Mallee town from the impact of that violent act affecting the world and our community. The candles to raise money for the surgery a little boy who'd suffered horrific burns in his African village was to have in Australia. There was a tangible sense of togetherness throughout the community during that time. It was as if people subconsciously acknowledged their vulnerability, united with a sense of gratitude for a safe place, regardless of their diverse cultural backgrounds.

Her eyes had lit up when she'd talked about her visit to a Christian community in India with a contingent of Australian parishioners. *They'd never met an Aboriginal Australian and bowed, to honour me. That's never happened to me in Australia.* I'd left her that day with an invitation to visit Sundarra with the feeling that she'd connect deeply to the land. After that we'd pass each other in town a few times and say hello and at the ecumenical service for peace the Catholic Church held with other denominations in the district, we hugged warmly. A week earlier we'd walked together in a Peace Walk down the main street with a handful of people, the Catholic parish priest and a family of five children each holding a placard with a letter spelling out PEACE.

I'd invited her to accept a peace candle for her community in the town centre park after the walk, but she humbly declined saying someone else would be more deserving of that honour. On the day, a shy frail Aboriginal woman gently guided by her, came forward to accept the flame. With trembling fingers, she held the miners lamp enclosing the flame and whispered with tear-filled eyes, *I never been given anything before.*

Her visit to Sundarra hasn't turned out the way I thought it would. We walk silently down to the creek, stay for a few moments, listen to sounds of nature, the breeze, the birds, the trickling water and the extraordinary feeling of sadness around us, then, looking slightly unsettled she turns and begins to walk the two kilometres back to the homestead. I follow, walking without a word, not knowing what she is feeling, sensing only she wants to leave.

Back at the homestead she drinks her tea and listens politely as I tell her about the covenant we'd made with Trust for Nature to protect the bushland. She nods in response but says nothing. Placing her cup on the table, not having touched the biscuits on her plate, she stands and calmly moves to the door.

We travel the two-kilometre track to the main highway in silence and hop out of the car to unlatch the farm gate pushing it wide open. Turning, I'm surprised to see her standing quite still beside the car, head slightly lifted, attentive, with a far-away look. She looks into me with deep amber eyes that speak more than words and says *They don't want you to go.*

At the end of that year, I leave Sundarra. Much later when I found time to reflect the wisdom dropped in – to truly listen means not only hearing but understanding with the heart. She'd made an impact on my life with few words which, had I truly listened, may have changed my destiny – the one responding to *They don't want you to go.*

Farewell

*Fare thee well; The elements be kind to thee, and make
thy spirits all of comfort.* Shakespeare

June 2005

A charismatic approachable Greek gentleman is Robinvale's mayor. He tells me the town has attracted more than forty different cultures – land and local business holders and mostly workers for the rich tapestry of agricultural holdings. A wander down the main street greets you with a variety of shops and business ventures catering for a multitude of multicultural needs: Greek, Italian, Serbian, Yugoslav, Indian, Filipino, Tongans, Asians and other representations from around the globe. The Aboriginal Co-op has pride of place in the township, built a few years before I arrived, caters for the First Nation people living in the large area of the Victorian Mallee country.

I love Sundarra and don't want to return to suburban life. I've found a special place with a vast ancient history, a land where every footstep tells a story: the giant river gums with carvings of Aboriginal artefacts, *middens* on higher ground, and in direct opposition the more recent history, ring-barked trees destroyed for all time by early white settlers clearing the land. In some places along the track to the Bonyaricall Creek and other parts of the terrain I experience deep feelings of peace, and in still others, unexplained sadness. No matter how many times I walk through these places the same feelings resurrect and persist.

As the Aboriginal elder had predicted months earlier, the land does not want to let me go. It takes two years to sell Sundarra. Sale contracts are signed then reneged on. Even the enormous moving van, thwarted in its efforts to remove our possessions from the homestead, gets bogged on the track in heavy rain – ironically, the rainfall breaking a three-year drought.

It took me at least five years to feel comfortable in my home town of Adelaide. I missed the dawns and sunsets of Sundarra but most of all I missed the sound of silence, when the land embraced me with its magic and the ancients spoke and welcomed me home.

Sundarra

Mallee country, stark like truth
entices nomads searching for the gilded prize
on cracked earth waiting with patient purpose,
for the sweet magic of cloud-full skies releasing nectar
into rivers, creeks, dams and into pipes of old gal' tanks.

Rusted carpets freed of wily winds turn green;
the earth refreshed, renewed, regenerated.

Gleeful gumboots slide to hopeful harvests
beneath a sky shaken from sleep.

Between veranda posts I sip a morning cuppa;
we celebrate with five-minute showers.

History

History is the witness of the times,
the torch of truth, the life of memory, the teacher of life,
the messenger of antiquity. Cicero

2023

Papacci's mandolin has another special place now, as it did in Sundarra, placed among prized artefacts from all over the world when he left it to me in his will. There it sat proudly on the rough-hewn wooden mantelpiece, the smooth sculpted body capturing the last rays of sun streaming into the yoga room from the wide curtain-less window. I'm not a musician, so it lay silent on the fireplace mantel bronzed by the sun slipping into the horizon and cooled by evening breezes wafting from open windows.

One evening I sit cross-legged on the floor watching the display of light stream over the mantelpiece above the vast brick fireplace and the mandolin breaks its silence. A twang with a distinctly earthy tone envelops the room, then another, then a light echoing trill. I'm both mystified and mesmerised by this symphony playing in the radiance of the setting sun. I listen bathed in shadow until the room is silent again, interspersed only by the call of a magpie settling for the night. The mandolin still has a voice that wants to be heard. I stand and gently lift the beautiful instrument my father's fingers had lovingly strummed for so many years off the wooden mantel, and, out of its middle hops a large slender cricket with a contoured body the shape and colour of the mandolin.

The mandolin is now suspended on the lounge room wall of my new suburban home with a black and gold cord which prompts another memory. It's from the giant birthday card I'd attached to the windscreen wipers of a small car I'd gifted my mother for her 75th birthday. Its as resplendent as ever alongside the faux fireplace in my new suburban home surrounded by creeks in a treed environment. The street tree across the road, a huge river gum remnant from ancient times is the only reminder of the mandolin's former country life.

In 2016 when I moved from my miniscule back garden in the suburbs and the Pidge who taught me so much, I found my reflections helped me gather the strength to create another reality – a new home and a new life. The view outside my window now would be lacking were it not for my thoughts colouring it with images beyond what is there.

From my writing room I see the garden, the only window in the house privileged to have this view. My garden is a happening place where nothing remains the same, continually in the throes of movement and change in one way or another. In the morning, and indeterminate other times during the day, the honey-eaters splashing with the gusto that defies their fragile, dainty frame, dive-bombing into the bird bath sitting on a decorative pedestal from the over-hanging fronds of the lemon tree. Feathers soaked to satisfaction they cling precariously to larger plants and flower petals, fluttering in joyful frenzies to dry their wings.

I counted thirteen in their little flock the other day, happiest and noisiest when together. The bird bath, surrounded by scruffy remnants of a once much-loved spring garden, borders a lawn. It's become a centrepiece confined by pots, large and small, boasting a variety of plants looking a little worse for wear, temporarily removed while the backyard receives a longawaited make-over. I'm hoping that before winter my dream of a wider view from my little writer's den will include a freestanding pergola, the old-fashioned kind, with a paraphernalia of coloured pots, festooned with greens and blooms of every description, hugging the wooden posts, poised and prolific. Then, I'll only need to open the sliding doors of my room when the mood strikes me, sit among the greenery and write with full view of my welcoming garden encouraging me to create visions from lost thoughts and dreams.

Meanwhile, the window still fixed and un-openable, is not yet a door. The pergola's four posts with unroofed beams await a final coat of paint, eucalyptus green, a shade to complement this piece of earth holding remnants of another's dreams and thoughts. I've never met the last owner but feel I know her by the bits and pieces she's left behind, settled in for the long haul, just like I have – in her eighties the real estate agent said.

Her garden constantly surprises me with new plants, blooms I don't even recognise – the more I water, the more they bloom. A bud here, a leaf there, some instantly familiar, others… weeds perhaps? She was a rose lover. Here and there they trail, neglected, and on a trellis in need of a coat of paint when I get round to it, perhaps eucalyptus green!

When my new friend, now my regular companion, and I came to the first *open*, the house embraced us. The home was filled with *olde worlde* touches which months on still lingered; above a china cabinet holding the dreams of our long-gone family, hung a painting she'd left behind – a landscape water colour in a silvery wooden frame, her name carefully signed at the bottom. In the small entrance hall, her four tiny china plates painted with delicate flower petals added an extra touch to our golden-framed wall mirror. It fitted perfectly between them, and anyhow, the decorative plates glued to the wall would probably have left holes if removed. Above the mantelpiece of our now refurbished fire-place, strangely real when the gas tongues lick the faux logs, sits a mirror in a twig-like frame where two life-like sparrows delicately perch.

It's nice to know that my home was once so loved, so much easier to add more creations. As for the mandolin, no-one in the family has yet accepted the challenge of playing it, but it is not silent. Every now and then Papacci speaks through it, twanging when least expected to remind my heart to sing of life's abundance.

ACKNOWLEDGEMENTS

Thank you to all the people past and present who have shared my life, inspired me to grow and made this book possible. My deepest gratitude to my husband Peter, my children and family who I continue to learn so much from. A reverent thank you to the Earth I stand on and the animals and elements continuing to bless and enrich my life. Anita Clara

REFERENCES
<u>Forty Thousand Quotations</u> – Charles Noel Douglas
Published by George G. Harrap & Co. Ltd. 1917
London Calcutta Sydney

<u>Bill the Bastard</u> (The story of Australia's greatest war horse) – Roland Perry
Published by Allen & Unwin 2012
Sydney Melbourne Auckland London

PHOTOGRAPHS
All photographs, including front and back covers,
are the property of the author

Also by Anita Clara Iussa:
Fragments in Time – A Diary of Homecoming (memoir)
Positively Short – A collection of feel-good tales
A Sense of Time – young adult novel
Beyond the Crystal – young adult novel
Fragments of a Life (memoir)

Author's Note
Many thanks to Rommie Corso of Hardshell Publishing who has not only supported my publishing journey but found herself unexpectedly in an encounter with the place where this memoir was written.
Moving next door to where I lived her attached garden
continues to inspire with the visitation of birds as mine had done.

writinganitaclaraiussa.com

Published by Anita Clara

Copyright © 2025. All rights reserved. No portion of this publication may be used, reproduced or transmitted by any means, digital, electronic, mechanical, photocopy or recording without written permission of the publisher, except in the case of brief quotations within critical articles or reviews.

ISBN: 978-0-6453821-2-9 (paperback)

First edition, 2025

For book orders and enquiries:
Email: counsel.u@bigpond.com
Web: writinganitaclaraiussa.com

 A catalogue record for this book is available from the National Library of Australia

www.ingramcontent.com/pod-product-compliance
Lightning Source LLC
Chambersburg PA
CBHW061757290426
44109CB00030B/2879